Foraging For Complete Beginners

Wilma .T Mill

Introduction

Embarking on a foraging journey in North America can be a rewarding adventure, and this book provides a comprehensive roadmap for those eager to explore the bounty of nature. The guide begins with Foraging 101, covering the basics that every beginner needs to know. Essential foraging tools are introduced to equip readers for their journey, emphasizing the importance of ethics and sustainability. Prioritizing safety is paramount, and the guide offers insights into navigating the outdoors responsibly.

Moving into Botany 101, readers gain valuable knowledge about the anatomy of plants. Understanding the various parts of plants, from flowers to mushrooms, lays the foundation for successful foraging. The guide emphasizes the importance of recognizing different plant parts, ensuring a safe and informed foraging experience.

From Plant to Plate, the guide delves into the diverse world of foraged foods. Mushrooms take center stage, with detailed information on various species and their characteristics. The exploration extends to flowers, fruits, shoots, shrubs, and nuts, providing a comprehensive overview of the edible treasures waiting to be discovered in North America.

Mushrooms, with their intriguing varieties, are explored in-depth, offering insights into identification, harvesting, and culinary applications. The guide then transitions to the world of flowers and fruits, showcasing a spectrum of edible possibilities in nature. Moving on to shoots, shrubs, and nuts, readers gain knowledge about diverse plant types, expanding their foraging repertoire.

Throughout the guide, an emphasis on responsible foraging practices and sustainability echoes, ensuring that foragers leave a positive impact on the environment. With a focus on plant identification, safety precautions, and ethical foraging, this book serves as a valuable companion for those venturing into the world of wild edibles.

Contents

FORAGING 101: BASICS

Foraging Tools: Equipping Yourself for the Road Ahead

Books will make up most of your expenses when it comes to foraging tools. The field guides, specifically the thicker encyclopedic variants, can cost a pretty penny. But luckily, you will not need much when you are out in the woods. Here are a few gears that can help you out.

A small knife: a jackknife or a pocket knife for cutting, snipping plants from their stems, branches, and roots

A small spade or trowel: for digging up rhizomes and tubers as well as mushrooms

Gloves: for that extra protection when handling potentially poisonous plants

A backpack: for storage of foraged items

A few bags: eco-bags, paper bags, or even plastic bags kept in your backpack for carrying and protecting foraged goods

Baskets: for foraged mushrooms and delicate flowers and leaves that cannot be crushed in the backpack

Magnifying glass: for looking at minuscule details to be 100% sure you are not ingesting a poisonous plant

Emergency rations: unexpected things may happen, and it is best to be prepared; pack a few food items with you

Clean water: for drinking

First aid kit

Ethics: The Rules of Foraging and Sustainability

For foragers, there is this thing called the foraging code of conduct. What is in the woods is not yours. Do not be greedy and pick everything you see. A good ratio would be to only harvest a third of what you see.

Let us say you see a patch of wild lavender - take only what you will be needing, and it should not go past a third of what is out there. Even if one might be so inclined to just harvest the whole patch, please restrain yourself. This is done because of 2 things: one of them is respect for other foragers that might come around and want to take some lavender too; the other is to give the plant a chance to propagate more.

When you harvest everything in a given place, you risk not seeing the plant grow next year. In short, you are lessening the chances of its survival. By only taking a third - and the next forager also only taking a third of what you leave and so on - there will always be something left of the plant.

Remember, over-harvesting has caused countless plants to go extinct. If the patch is really small, better move on to the next area. Never take the last one.

Know what plants are endangered. If you see a plant that is already labeled as "at-risk," refrain from taking them. By law, it is illegal to pick endangered species. If there is a chance to cultivate them in your yard or garden, do so. The ginkgo nuts survived for centuries because of human cultivation.

Do not damage or trample any other plants on your way to forage something else. Do not destroy a plant's natural habitat.

Use a knife or a pair of shears when cutting parts of the plant. Excessive use of physical force may damage it, or worse, uproot it.

And lastly, be fully aware of the legal side. It's always best to know where you are foraging. I would not worry if it is on your own property, but if it is a ginkgo tree on the side of the road in the suburbs, I would ask the owners first for permission before picking. Technically, there is a law that states that foraging from lands that are not one's own is not theft, as long as you do not earn any money or gain any reward from it. Do not forage from nature reserves or other protected areas. Do not forage from botanical gardens.

Safety First

As a beginner to foraging, I will not tell you that you need to learn to identify all plants and flowers. You are not a botanist, and neither am I.

Still, I believe that you should know your area like the back of your hand. Metaphorically speaking, it's like knowing the old house you grew up in - you must be familiar enough to know what floor boards to avoid, where the water leaks when it rains, and what shutters rattle in the wind.

So before you can think about foraging, I urge you to walk around your area first and be familiar with it. Walk around and take a mental note of where everything is resting. Next, you need to try to identify the various flora and fauna around where you live - that skill should come first. There's no need to know everything at the beginning of this journey. Uncover the stones one by one.

For a beginner, you need only know about the plants around you - the ones that are easiest to identify and those that you are sure are 100% edible. It will take years of study and a Ph.D. to know everything about plants, and one doesn't need that in order to find the simple pleasures of foraging. So, I say it is best to learn along the way. There's no shame in starting with the easiest, safest, and most identifiable plants in your backyard.

For this, I would suggest that you go out and walk around your area first with a field guide, a magnifying glass, your camera or smartphone, and a handy notebook or a sketchpad in tow. Walk around and feel at home first, then make a note and try to identify the plants and mushrooms you see. It is an exercise to train your eye and your mind to get used to seeing these plants and mushrooms in a new light.

When you start your journey with foraging, being detail-oriented can come a long way. Our kids have drawn a wonderfully whimsical map of the manor and the area surrounding it for their own adventures, foraging or otherwise. They made notes on where the flowers bloom, on what path to stay on for the best mushrooms, and where the prettiest flowers are. One of the docents we have in the manor for the historical tours saw it, and now visitors are welcome to get a copy of the children's map for our regular "foraging parties."

There are various "foraging parties" being hosted if you know where to look. For instance, if you visit us in the manor, we will gladly take you along during one of our foraging trips in and around the woods in the area before the dinner bell rings.

So look at the various shapes and colors of the plants you come across. Does it have flowers? How do the leaves look? Look at the veins. Where does it grow? How did it grow? Be inquisitive like a child and compare it to your field guide. Look at all the characteristics of every plant or fungi you come across. Your field guide will be your closest companion during your trips.

On field guides, some will have photographs, while some will have detailed botanical illustrations. But my wife and I actually favor the ones with the botanical illustrations. Call it what you will - maybe it is part of managing the manor, or maybe the Victorian spirit of the house has rubbed off on us, but we like the quaint vintage look of the illustrations. It's also the most useful if you absolutely want to get a detailed picture of the plant or fungi you are identifying.

You see, pictures are great, and the macro shots are breathtaking, but with illustrations, every detail is drawn there for a reason. Every strand of fur or hair is there to help you positively identify these plants and mushrooms. A lot of plants and mushrooms look the same, so having a keen eye and a handy and detailed field guide will work for your best interest when you are just starting out.

There are various field guides available, but be sure to choose the book that is the most accurate representation of your area's plant life. A book about sub tropical flora and fauna will be of no use to you if you live in a temperate zone.

In the end, what you want to achieve is the sort of familiarity you have when you are choosing produce in the store. You will never mistake an apple for an orange in your local grocer, will you?

BOTANY 101: OF PLANTS AND PARTS

You should also know the basics about plants. We, as children, were taught basic biology at school. We were taught about the different parts of the plant and the seasons, as well as the different types of soil, rocks, and environment. Still, I really doubt if anyone ever remembers everything school taught us back in grade school. If knowledge over a subject matter is not regularly used, it will lie dormant. So before you can start foraging, I suggest that you refresh your memory about biology. It will also come in handy when reading field guides to know what a stamen and a lenticel are.

Parts of Plants

Leaf margin: the outer perimeter of the leaf; the leaf edges

Ovate: leaves that are shaped like an oblong, oval, egg-shaped

Lobed: leaves with deeply indented margins or edges

Rounded: leaves that are circular in shape

Sagittate: leaves that are shaped like arrows or spades

Cordate: leaves that are heart-shaped

Palmate: leaves that radiate from a single central common point, like the palm of a hand; maple leaves

Pinnate: leaves that have divisions or leaflets arranged on opposite sides of the stem; palm leaves

Serrated or toothed: jagged leaf edges that are reminiscent of the blades of a hand saw

Simple leaves: a leaf that is not divided into leaflets; a single leaf

Compound leaves: leaves that have more than one smaller leaves attached

Leaflet: a small leaf that is part of a compound leaf; it is not borne or sprouting from the main branch but from a branch of a leaf or a petiole

Alternate: single leaves that sprout or are borne along a stem at different levels or alternately

Opposite: single leaves that grow opposite each other separated by the stem

Dissected: leaves that are divided into numerous smaller leaves; like ferns

Rhizome: a fleshy stem that grows underground horizontally that can produce shoots and root systems for a new plant; it stores starch and protein as the plant's food source; potatoes, ginger

Runner: a thinner or slender stem that runs parallel to the ground; it can produce roots and stems; strawberries

---

Flowers

Petals: the other part of the flower that encloses or surrounds the stamen and pistil

Stamen: a flower's male reproductive organ: includes the pollen, anther, and the filament

Pistil: a flower's female reproductive organ: includes the ovary, stigma, and style

Sepals: the leaf-like structure on the underside of the flower that holds and protects the flower bud

Stigma: the sticky part of the flower's female reproductive organ that catches the pollen that falls from the anther; this starts the reproduction process

Anther: part of the flower's male reproductive organ; sits atop the filament and holds the pollen

Pollen: microspores that fall onto the stigma that carries the male genetic material of the flower

Style: the stalk of the flower's female reproductive organ that connects the stigma to the ovary

Ovary: the portion at the base of the flower that is part of the flower's female reproductive organ; inside the ovary are ovules that develop into seeds; the ovary itself will develop into a fruit.

Mushroom

Fruiting body: commonly, the umbrella-shaped body of the mushroom that is above ground; includes the stem, ring, spores, gills, and cap

Mycelium: the root system of the mushroom; it commonly forms underground and out of sight; an example of a mycelium that's visible is the chaga mushroom

Cap: the topmost part and the most recognizable part of the mushroom; it protects the spore-producing parts of the mushroom

Gills: thin, platelike structure that is commonly on the underside of the mushroom; it produces and contains the spores responsible for the mushroom's propagation

Spores: it is the microscopic, unicellular reproductive cells of the mushroom; once dispersed and it finds a host, it can germinate and produce mycelium that turns into a new mushroom

Ring / partial veil: a thin piece of mushroom tissue that protected and covered the gills when the mushroom was still young

Stem: the mushroom body that supports the cap and connects it to the mycelium

Volva / universal veil: a piece of mushroom tissue that protected the mushroom during its infancy; as the mushroom grows, the cap breaks through the volva

FROM PLANT TO PLATE

Mushrooms

Out here in the country, partly because of the weather, mushrooms are plentiful - and after just a few days of rain, along the paths in the woods, pretty little mushrooms can be seen peeping up from the soil and moss. On such days, I send the kids out with baskets to pick out mushrooms. The kids are familiar with the woods at the back of the farm, as this is also where we hold our occasional mushroom foraging parties for guests in the manor.

As most of you might know, mushrooms are a part of the fungus kingdom, which are numbered around 2.2 to 3.8 million species. With that staggering amount, mushrooms are only a part of it, and an even smaller percentage of these are edible - approximately 600 species of mushrooms are edible. So it's a good idea not to eat every mushroom that you might see when you're out foraging. For beginners - and I even tell these to the guests - it's better to stick to what you know are 100% edible.

Mushrooms come in many shapes and forms. What people usually call the "mushroom" is actually the fruiting body of the entire organism. Underneath, you can find a root system called mycelium, which is made up of a dense network of thin filaments called hyphae. If you are unsure of the mushroom you are harvesting and you would like to better identify it, it is sometimes better to dig deeper and pry out some of the mycelia. Paying close attention to their shape, color, gills, spores, and where they grow from can help you pinpoint which mushrooms are safe for eating or not.

Since a lot of mushrooms are poisonous and even deadly, to be safe, please do not try to eat mushrooms that have not been properly identified by an expert. Also, keep in mind that all wild mushrooms should be cooked first before you can think about eating them. Even edible mushrooms, especially the wild ones, can cause an upset stomach. So I suggest just eating a small cooked piece first just to be safe.

That said, with all 600 plus species of edible mushrooms out there for your picking, this book cannot possibly teach you how to identify them all. Thankfully, there are other books for that, so I will just aim to equip you with the basics to get you started.

CHICKEN OF THE WOODS

Chicken of the woods (*Laetiporus sulphureus*) is also known as a sulfur shelf, chicken mushroom, or chicken fungus - it's a bracket type fungi and would grow from dead or dying hardwood trees; thus, they are considered to be parasitic. These mushrooms will not grow unless the whole tree has been infected, causing the white mycelium to grow and be visible in the cracks of the tree while bringing about a reddish-brown heart rot.

Characteristics: The fruit body does not have a stem leaving only the cap with shapes that vary from irregular to semicircular and fan-like. It is also suede-like to touch with a wrinkled to smooth texture. The cap measures around 5 to 30 cm by 20 cm with a thickness of 3 cm.

When young, these are bright yellow or orange with thick and watery flesh. However, that color will fade as the mushroom matures, leaving a tougher fruit body that will eventually dry up and crumble away. The growth can range from very large but few fronds on the side of the trees to a smallish cluster of little shelves.

Spore print: The spore prints for this mushroom are usually light yellow or white, but they can be a little hard to get as the caps are not as prominent as in the other mushrooms. There are no gills, but there are small tubes found under the brackets - circular or oval, around 2 to 3 mm by 15 to 30 mm deep.

Environment: During the summer, fall, and sometimes even spring seasons, chicken of the woods can be found growing in large clusters around the trunk and the base of hardwood trees like oaks (mostly), beech, or cherry. Since these mushrooms are parasitic, they are known to mostly grow in dying or rotting trees, but it is not uncommon to find them growing in living trees too.

White chicken of the woods rot the butt wood so they can be found growing at the base of dead and dying trees. While the yellow chicken of the woods, on the other hand, rot the heartwood, so these grow on the trunk of these trees. However, those that can be found growing on eucalyptus, yews, and conifers should be avoided as the mushroom may absorb the oils natural to these trees, which can cause problems when harvested and eaten.

Although abundant in the US, Canada, and Europe, these are also easily found in some parts of Asia.

Taste Profile: The name of this mushroom comes from, you guessed right, the taste. A majority would say that it tastes like chicken, hence the name. But to others, it is meaty and has a slight lemony tang to it, while others are reminded of crabs and lobsters. Although people might argue about the taste of this certain mushroom, the texture of this when cooked is inarguably meat-like and can thus be used to mimic the mouthfeel of meat.

Harvesting and usage: For best results, collect young chicken of the woods for your recipes while they are still young and tender. There will be no need to harvest the mature ones as you will undoubtedly find them very unpalatable - they are tough and will taste like wood or sawdust even when boiled for hours. That said, even with the young ones, it will be better to use the edges as the mushroom tends to get thicker and the flesh tougher as it gets to the center. However, if you do plan to use the whole mushroom for your recipes, the center would need to be boiled in water for over an hour to be palatable.

As a rule, good and tender chicken of the woods, when cut, should produce yellow or milky juices. Check for the colors - they should be bright, and no bugs should be clinging onto the fronds.

For longer storage, you can keep cooked chicken of the woods frozen in vacuum-sealed bags. Sadly, dehydration will affect the taste of the mushroom. The polypore structure of this mushroom - located on the underside of the shelves or fronds - hardens into a denser material when dried, making the mushroom taste like wood and be tougher, very much like a mature mushroom would.

Recipe: Simply Sauteed Chicken of the Woods

Chicken of the woods mushroom

Olive oil

Butter

Garlic (chopped)

A quarter of an onion (chopped)

Salt

2 to 3 tablespoons of wine (we like to use sake, but rice wine or white wine is fine as well as cooking wine)

Black pepper

1. Prepare and cut chicken of the woods into smaller, manageable chunks. We like to slice them into long thin strips around an inch wide. Place a skillet on medium heat and pour olive oil in. When the oil is hot enough, fry up the chicken of the woods until browned on both sides. Drain them of oil and set them aside. On the same skillet, melt the butter in low heat and toss in the chopped garlic and onion; sauté until lightly browned and fragrant.

2. Add the browned chicken of the woods back in the skillet. Pour in the wine and mix the ingredients together until the wine starts simmering slightly. Season with salt and pepper, then serve.

GIANT PUFFBALL MUSHROOM

Giant Puffball Mushrooms (Calvatia gigantea), or just giant puffball, is another common form of mushroom usually found during the late summer and autumn months in fields, meadows, and deciduous forests. A form of puffball mushroom, this is a great mushroom for beginners as the fully grown one is big enough and the shape unique enough that there would be less danger of mistaking it for another rather poisonous mushroom.

Characteristics: As the name suggests, it is a giant when compared to other mushrooms. It can grow up to anywhere between 10 to 90 cm in diameter normally, but occasionally you can find one that can reach around 150 cm in diameter too. With that size, it is not surprising that it can weigh up to 20 kg. When young, they are white in color, and the bigger ones can be easily mistaken as volleyballs when spotted in the fields. As the mushroom matures, it will turn brown and will be inedible. And sometimes, at this stage, it can be rather poisonous as it will develop millions of spores that will be released as the matured skin cracks. The spores released from mature puffball mushrooms were used before by the native people as an anticoagulant for wounds.

Spore print: There are no gills, but the spore print for this mushroom is olive-brown, and you can easily get it from a mature mushroom.

Environment: You can easily see Giant Puffball Mushrooms in the edges of meadows, fields, and woodlands during the summer and fall seasons in the US, Canada, and Europe, and some parts of Asia. These mushrooms thrive on nutrient-rich waste grounds as they feed on dead organic matter.

Taste Profile: The edible part of the Giant Puffball Mushroom is its inner flesh. Young ones will have white flesh that is not dissimilar to tofu or marshmallows. The taste is mild and, when toasted and properly browned in a skillet or an oven, will taste nutty and earthy, like a good mushroom would. Remember, the inner flesh should be white - if it is any other color, it is not edible. The mouthfeel of this particular mushroom is strange for many, making it not so popular among the uninitiated. It is soft and spongy, especially when not properly prepared.

Harvesting and usage: Giant puffball mushrooms are not the only puffball mushrooms out there. Keep in mind that the edible ones will have white, solid flesh inside. If you are unsure, cut it open. It should not have gills. Refrain from harvesting the smaller ones as these can be easily confused with other smaller poisonous mushrooms like the Amanita or the pigskin puffball, which has a harder, rougher skin and a black or purple interior flesh. But the giant puffballs ones will not look like any other poisonous mushrooms, so they should be safe for beginners.

Harvest only the younger mushrooms. A good giant puffball mushroom, when cut open, should be pure white, very much like the color of cream cheese with the texture of firm tofu. Also, make sure the inner flesh is free from any traces of insect infestation. The flesh should be firm; if it is spongy and too soft, refrain from eating it.

It is easy enough to prepare; first, dust off any dirt and debris. If the skin is clean and tender, you can go ahead and eat the skin, too; otherwise, peel the skin off. It should come off fairly easily. Do not wash this mushroom as it will act like a sponge and absorb too much water and thus make it too soggy for eating. And unlike the chicken of the woods, the giant puffball mushroom can be dehydrated and rehydrated without any issues. What we like to do, on the other hand, is to slice them up and lay them out on a piece of parchment paper and freeze them. Afterward, when all the individual pieces have been frozen, place them in a Ziplock and then back in the freezer.

For some, these puffball mushrooms are best when coated, breaded, and deep-fried. The crispy golden fried breading cancels out the soggy, sponge-like texture of the mushroom. But here in the manor, one of the best-loved dishes by our guests is the relatively simple stir-fried puffball mushrooms with seasonal vegetables and plants from our farm.

Recipe: Egg-y Puffball Toast

Giant puffball mushroom

Olive oil or butter

3 eggs (1 egg beaten)

¼ cup of milk

Salt

Pepper

Chives (chopped)

Various herbs from your garden (we like to use a mix of basil and thyme)

1. Peel your puffball mushroom. Slice them like you would a loaf of bread an inch thick. If your mushroom is big, feel free to slice them into a manageable size that can fit your skillet.

2. In a bowl, mix the beaten egg along with the milk. Season the mixture with a dash of salt. Get your skillet and get it hot enough. Pour a few tablespoons of olive oil into it or if you want, melt a pat of butter for a richer taste. When your oil or butter is hot enough, dip your puffball mushrooms into your prepared egg mixture and place it on your skillet. Fry both sides until they are lightly browned. Drain of oil and set aside.

3. In the same skillet, fry up some eggs, sunny side up (depending on how you want your yolks - we want ours very runny). Place these fried eggs on top of your mushrooms and season with salt, pepper, and a dash of fresh herbs. Serve.

HEN OF THE WOODS MUSHROOM

Hen of the Woods Mushroom (*Grifola frondosa*), as it's more popularly called in the US and Canada, is also called more famously by its Japanese name, *Maitake* or *kumotake* (it's a bracket type mushroom). But depending on where you are in the world, it is also called sheep's head, ram's head, *signorina* in Italy, and *laubporling* in Germany. It's a popular mushroom featured in a lot of cuisines all over the world, especially in Asia, where it's treated as a medicinal mushroom that can help with diabetes and hypertension. Its extracts are used as dietary supplements that are sometimes marketed as a treatment for diabetes, HIV, and cancer.

This is also one of the most distinguishable mushrooms you can pick if you are a beginner, as there are no poisonous mushrooms you can mistake it with. And if there are any look-alikes, all are edible, like the chicken of the woods, another bracket-type mushroom, and the black staining polypore (*Meripilus sumstinei*).

Also easily cultivated, Hen of the woods can be easily found being sold in your local green grocer. Cultivated Maitake is relatively cheap, but you will find that wild-harvested maitakes can be sold at a much higher price point.

Characteristics: Hen of the woods mushrooms grow out of just a single white central stem - this stem branches out to form clusters topped with caps that can measure to 30 cm in height. The main fruit body can grow to be 10 to 100 cm across and should be composed of a cluster of flattened caps which curl around, forming a shape of a spoon with wavy edges.

Colored a dull sort of brownish grey color, the caps have a tendency to lighten or fade slowly to white towards the center, with each growing from a size of 2 to 10 cm across with a thickness of just .5 cm to 1 cm - a lot of times even thinner.

Hen of the woods is a polypore. On the underside of the cap, tiny pores or tubes are packed closely together with 2 to 3 pores per 1 mm - and upon closer inspection, these tubes will have a depth of 3 mm at their deepest. The pore surface will be colored a light grey when it's younger. This color will gradually fade to white as the mushroom matures while at the same time showing a bit of brown and yellow undertones as it gets older. From the underside, you can see that the cluster of stems and caps will remind you of the structure easily found in cauliflowers and broccoli.

When seen from afar, the shape and the color of this mushroom can easily make it look like a sitting hen, thus its name here in the US. In Japan, you can find Maitake mushrooms that can grow as heavy as 45 kg, thus earning the rightful nickname King of mushrooms.

Spore print: Hen of the woods' spore print is white. It is a polypore, so you can get your spore prints from the pores or tubes on the undersides of the caps.

Environment: Hen of the woods mushrooms are easily found during the fall months, from August to the end of November, and can be found in the northern temperate forests of the US and in the eastern parts of Canada. It is also found growing all over Europe, the northeastern part of Japan, and China.

It is a parasitic type of mushroom, which means that like chicken of the woods, the Hen of the Woods mushroom also thrives on dead or dying trees, but it can also be known to fruit from living trees. It favors oak trees, but a lot could be found growing on the base of elm and maple trees too. It would be prudent to make a note of these trees for future mushroom hunts as maitake has a tendency to grow again on the same spot when the next fall season comes around.

Taste Profile: The Hen of the woods is a mushroom prized for its taste, with its strong earthy and meaty taste with a slight hint of spice. I like it best when it's dehydrated and crunchy. The missus loves this mushroom - the guests also love it, and it is a much loved regular in the autumn menu we serve in the manor.

Harvesting and usage: The Hen of the woods is pretty easy to harvest. It usually pops out easily when you pull it out from the base of an oak or any hardwood trees, but bring with you a small pocket knife for that singular, giant maitake that you might actually find. On a very large maitake, the stems can grow very thick, so a knife might be useful to lessen the risk of damaging the mushroom. If the maitake you manage to find is a bit older, only cut off the top part where the fronds or caps are still young and tender.

These mushrooms like wet environments; they also like to blend in with the fallen leaves of autumn at the base of large oaks. You will find that after a particularly heavy rain is the best time to go hunting for these mushrooms during the maitake season. We have our own oak tree growing by the edge of the forest, and it usually grows out a big head of Maitake every year. And if you know of a copse of oak trees near your area, make a pilgrimage to it during the autumn months and poke around the base of these magnificent trees. The brown color inherent to these mushrooms might make them harder to find, but the curly fronds will be a dead giveaway.

These mushrooms are short-lived and are the best tasting when they are young and tender. When cut crosswise, the flesh inside should be firm and white. As the mushroom matures, it will start to smell unpleasant and will turn out to taste very bitter and woody.

When preparing the maitake, it's best to just use or cut out the top part where it's relatively clean and still young. It is best to prepare it like you would a giant head of cauliflower or broccoli since the

21

structures are relatively the same. From the underside of the mushroom, slice so that sections can be separated and you can see through the branching stems and caps. Check for any signs of bugs. When the mushrooms are cut into manageable chunks that are suited for cooking, wash them thoroughly in water.

The hen of the woods is a mushroom that works well when dehydrated and rehydrated. There's no loss in taste. The dehydrated mushrooms are crispy and can be eaten as is, like chips or appetizers or even added into soups for that extra punch of umami. Otherwise, it is great in all manner of cooking, in soups, stews, stir-fries, and baked in the oven.

Recipe: Maitake Cheesy Toast

Maitake or hen of the woods mushroom

3 cloves of garlic (chopped)

Butter

Salt

Ground black pepper

Bread

Cheese (any quick melting cheese; we use a mix of shredded cheeses in the manor: mozzarella, provolone, and Swiss)

1. Heat the skillet. When it's hot enough, melt 2 pats of butter and add in the chopped garlic. Sauté until it is tender and lightly browned. Then toss in the chopped maitake mushrooms.

2. Sauté the mushrooms in garlic until it's tender and season with salt and pepper. I like to add in a small bit of soy sauce at this point.

Take the skillet off the heat.

3. Spread butter on a piece of bread and lightly toast it. After your bread is warm and toasty, scoop a spoonful of the garlicky mushroom on top of the bread. Pile them on the bread until it is about an inch thick, then place the cheeses on top.

4. Place this in an oven toaster for 5 minutes or until all the cheeses have melted. Serve while hot.

CHANTERELLE MUSHROOM

Chanterelle mushrooms (*Cantharellus cibarius*) are one of the most recognizable mushrooms sought after by food lovers and chefs because of their taste. Also known as golden chanterelles, these mushrooms can be found scattered all across the forests of North America, growing in solitude or in groups. It is also one of the most prolific mushrooms, with over 40 varieties of this tasty mushroom in North America alone.

Characteristics: Chanterelles are quite easy to identify, but recognizing between different varieties is another matter. The most common distinguishing feature of a chanterelle mushroom is its cap, funnel-shaped or vase-like, with an irregular margin that can measure up to 10 cm in diameter. From the stem up to its cap, it is usually measured at 6 to 9 cm on average.

Its colors range from a light yellow to the deep yellow of egg yolks. These are quite easy to spot as they pop out directly from the soil amid the forest floor, mostly scattered around growing individually. These are not saprobic types of fungi, meaning they don't grow on dead trees and stumps, unlike its toxic look-alike, the Jack O'lantern mushroom.

Many people mistake the Jack O'lantern with the chanterelle as they do look similar in some ways, but the Jack O'lantern should be avoided at all costs. It is not a deadly mushroom, but it will cause you great intestinal distress if you do ingest it. The Jack O'lantern is a saprobic type of mushroom. It is like the chicken of the woods and the maitake in the sense that it grows on dead trees and stumps, but it does occasionally grow away from these dead trees - probably a foot away or so.

Even so, the mycelium is still getting nourishment from the buried dead tree roots. They also grow in dense clusters, around 12 or more, all connected at the tapered base. The chanterelles, on the other hand, more often than not, would grow individually by themselves. And if they do form clusters, these will only contain 4 to 5 caps or less.

Another big difference is their gills - the chanterelle mushrooms do have gills, but some field guides call them "fake gills." This should be a telltale sign, too, as the Jack O'lantern has a more pronounced individual plate or blade-like gills that you would usually associate with mushrooms in general.

These plate-like gills would be packed close to each other and would taper town to their connected bases. These gills can easily be pulled off with tweezers. The chanterelles differ widely by having blunt ridges or folds that are forked or cross veined in between, tapering down along the stem. Compared to the Jack O'lantern gills, the chanterelle gills are more like thick ridges that are attached firmly to the cap and will be difficult to pull apart.

Another thing to note would be their smell - chanterelles, in general, would smell fruity, and many say that it smells vaguely like an apricot. The Jack O'lantern, on the other hand, smells like a mushroom would - earthy and woodsy.

Spore print: The spore print of the chanterelle is a pale pinkish yellow to white (it's yellow for Jack O'lantern mushrooms).

Environment: The chanterelle mushrooms are mycorrhizal fungi, growing directly from the soil, not on trees. They start popping out of the soil from late summer to around early fall. It would be a good idea to look for hardwood trees in your area when foraging for chanterelles. Looking for areas that have trees like oak, maple, poplar, and white oak would be a good way to start.

If recently, your area has been drenched by a lot of rain followed by a wave of heat, you can go out and look for chanterelle mushrooms on the forest floors after a few days. The natural humidity under the trees and between taller grasses is a natural habitat for these tasty mushrooms as they like the damp. You can mostly find them under the shade of trees, grasses, and in low-lying areas near streams and run-offs, as these mushrooms love the moisture and shade.

Taste Profile: Chanterelles have a taste profile that is often said to be difficult to describe. And owing to the 400 plus varieties we can find here in the US, it is only but natural that the taste will vary between each variety slightly. More often than not, chanterelles are described to be very rich in flavor with a fruity smell that can remind you of apricots with some varieties. The golden chanterelle among the varieties is the one that is most favored for its taste around the world. Considered to be a gourmet mushroom, they rank high up there beside truffles and morels.

Harvesting and usage: Once you find a colony of these rather tasty treats, it would be a good idea to look over the entire area as you are bound to find more of them. Leave the smaller and younger ones alone if you know there will be more rain to come. More are expected to pop up after a good drenching. Be careful when you tread on the forest floor when you do find a scattering of chanterelles for fear of damaging the mycelium that is usually spread out on the soil.

When cleaning, separate the mushrooms by hand and brush away any dirt or debris. Again look for signs of bug damage. When cut crosswise, the chanterelle mushroom's interior flesh is of a white color, reminiscent of that of string cheese. Meanwhile, Jack O'lantern mushrooms' interior flesh is colored yellow-orange.

A batch of fresh chanterelle mushrooms will keep in a paper bag for 10 days. Otherwise, it is best to use a fresh bag immediately after foraging. You can also cook and then freeze them, but these mushrooms do very well when dried or dehydrated for storage. In fact, you can find chefs that say dehydrated chanterelles will have a deeper taste profile than fresh ones - but mind you, doing so would make the mushroom chewier when rehydrated.

Recipe: Rustic Chanterelle Pasta

Chanterelle mushroom (broken apart and cleaned)

Pasta

olive oil

3 cloves of garlic (sliced thinly)

Parmesan cheese

Salt

Pepper

1. Pour water into a large pot and let it boil. Once boiling, drop your pasta in. Let it boil until al dente, then drain the pasta, keeping some of the pasta water separate.

2. While the pasta is cooking, heat a skillet. When your skillet is hot enough, pour 2 tablespoons or so of olive oil. Wait until the oil is hot, then throw the sliced garlic in. Sauté lightly until garlic is tender, keeping an eye on the flame. The garlic must not be burned. When the garlic starts to smell fragrant, toss in the chanterelle mushrooms. Lightly sauté until the mushroom is cooked and coated in garlic oil.

3. Place the cooked pasta in with the garlic chanterelle mushroom. Toss the pasta around until every strand is thoroughly coated in garlic oil. Season with salt and pepper. If the pasta looks like it is too dry, add in the pasta water you have set aside earlier.

4. Turn off the heat. While the pasta and the skillet are still hot, pour in the grated parmesan cheese and swirl it around with the pasta until thoroughly melted. Serve while hot with a garnish of herbs of your choice.

CHAGA MUSHROOM

Chaga mushroom (*Inonotus Obliquus*) is a very recognizable fungus that grows on birch trees in the northern parts. A member of the *Hymenochaetaceae* family, it is a parasitic type of mushroom that preys on birch trees. Recently over the years, the popularity of this mushroom has surged due to its purported medicinal properties. It is very popular in parts of Asia and Eastern Europe, but now people in our hemisphere are starting to understand the value of this mushroom, too.

Characteristics: A chaga mushroom may not look like a mushroom, and you can easily walk past it in the forest if you don't know what you are looking for. But it is widely recognizable, and once you do know what to look for, you can immediately spot it.

A fully grown chaga will be around 25 to 40 cm across and will generally protrude out of the tree up to 30 cm. It will have no usual shape, but the most distinguishable feature of the chaga mushroom is its outer surface. Colored black like charcoal and looking like charcoal, it is most noticeable as it will be protruding out of the tree. This protrusion is the sterile conk and is made up of a mass of the mushroom's mycelium that is called the sclerotium. It will have a hard, cracked, and rough texture on the outside, and when cut open, the inside flesh is like that of a cork - softer and amber-colored.

Contrary to popular belief, this is not the fruiting body of the mushroom. The fruiting body of the mushroom is not usually visible as it is found inside the tree.

Spore print: The spores of the chaga mushroom are under the bark of the tree near the sclerotium. When the host tree starts to die, the spores will begin to disperse in the air and will look for a new host tree. The spores will enter through a wound on the tree, where it will take root and start anew.

Environment: Chaga mushrooms take longer to grow, so you are most likely to find them in older birch trees, but it is not unknown to grow on the younger trees as well. The most common hosts are the paper birch and the yellow birches. A developed chaga is typically found on birch trees over 40 years old and will favor the colder climates in Northern Canada, Alaska, Northern Europe, Russia, Siberia, and Korea.

Taste Profile: It may look like burnt tree bark, but chaga does not taste like one. Although it cannot be eaten as it is like a culinary mushroom - it is too rough and fibrous - the taste is surprisingly mild, fruity, and a little sweet. It has the same compounds you can usually find in vanilla beans, so you can sometimes taste a bit of vanilla in your chaga tea.

If the chaga you have tastes bitter and off, it will be better to not drink it. The bitterness might be a sign that the mushroom has been spoiled, or worse, contaminated.

Harvesting and usage: Although it is very tempting for some beginners to lop off the entire protrusion when they come across a chaga mushroom in the woods, please refrain from doing so. Cutting off a part of the sclerotium from particularly large and matured chaga will be sufficient for you and your family for years. Removing the whole protrusion will kill the tree. Do keep in mind that the tree and the mushroom are finite resources, and recently there have been problems of people being unwise enough to remove the entire thing. If you are harvesting, take only what you need and leave at least 25% of the sclerotium attached to the tree.

To harvest this mushroom, you will need a smaller axe and find a living tree with the telltale protrusion. The outer skin is as hard as wood, and you will need to hit the most outer part of the protrusion at an angle. Wedge the ax in an inch or so and slowly work the ax until the chopped bit can come loose.

Unlike other mushrooms, chaga cannot be eaten as is. It will need to be dried out and ground down into powder form before it can be added to meals or be made into tea. Using a dehydrator will work, but it can be easily done by leaving the chaga out to dry in the sun and air for 3 days. During that period, it will start to crack. Larger chunks of dried chaga can be great for tea.

Recipe: Chaga Tea

In order to properly extract all the purported benefits of chaga, you will need to leave it simmering in hot water for 10 to 15 minutes. Hot boiling water poured from a kettle onto the chaga will not be able to extract all of its wonderful medicinal qualities. But it is not unheard of to leave pieces of chaga boiling in water for an hour or more.

It is best to drink the tea while it is still hot and freshly brewed, but you can leave it in the fridge for about 7 days if you like. Powdered chaga can also be added to smoothies, soups and could also be taken as a supplement when it's in a capsule.

CREMINI MUSHROOM

The cremini mushroom, scientifically known as *Agaricus bisporus,* is an edible mushroom native to Europe and North America. It is one of the popular mushroom types for those who are into foraging, although its kind has been diminishing in the wild. The reason for its popularity sprouts from the fact that the mushroom does not depend on seasons. It grows at any time of the year as long as the conditions for its growth are met.

The cremini comes in two colors; white and brown, with each having a unique name while young and different names while mature. For the common man, the cremini is just that, and there is no need to break down the subgenres and names for the mushroom. This mushroom can easily be identified thanks to its round closed caps that are mostly brown when mature.

Characteristics: Cremini mushrooms do not grow very tall. They grow in clusters of short, about three-inch stalks with closed caps. The round, smooth, closed cap will help you easily identify the mushroom if you spot it in the wild. As they get older, most cremini mushrooms tend to turn darker as compared to white mushrooms. They are loved for their complex flavor that beats most mushroom species discussed in this book.

Edible Parts: As is the case with other types of mushroom, the cremini is edible wholly except for the roots. The stem and the round caps are suitable for eating since they are not poisonous. They can be eaten either raw or cooked, although the cooked version is the best. Raw ones may harbor bacteria or contamination from the area where they are found.

Environment Where Found: If you are into growing the mushrooms in your garden, first look at the requirements based on the areas where they grow. Generally, these mushrooms are native to European and Northern American grasslands. Originally they had grey-colored caps with broad flat scales. Due to evolution and breeding, modern-day cremini mushrooms can grow in most places in the US and are quite different in appearance.

The beauty of cremini mushrooms is that they do not depend on seasons. They can grow at any time of the day as long conditions are met. They thrive in warm and wet conditions. Due to these requirements, they are common along the American coast in the south but also grow in other parts. You can plant them at home as long as you provide the ideal conditions.

Taste Profile: The cremini mushroom has a meaty and earthy flavor that is quite intense as compared to the white mushrooms. The meaty flavor of the mushroom comes out when cooked, even though it can be served raw. It is a great substitute for white mushroom, even though it is much harder to come by.

Harvesting and Usage: Cremini mushrooms can be harvested easily by plucking them out of the ground. However, in cases where the mushroom is stuck to the ground, plucking may lead to damage. In this case, you may use a small knife to cut it at the base. Harvesting the cremini mushrooms requires a lot of care since they can easily get damaged in the process. They should ideally be harvested in the morning or late evenings after the sun goes down.

Recipe: Garlic Butter Mushrooms

There are many recipes that work with Cremini mushrooms. You could prepare them in the same manner you prepare white mushrooms. You can make yours with stew or follow a custom recipe for a much tasty meal. Below is one of my favorite mushroom recipes you may want to try out.

4 teaspoons of melted butter

2 cloves of garlic

2 teaspoons of freshly chopped thyme

1 teaspoon of balsamic vinegar

a pinch of kosher salt

Freshly ground black pepper

1lb of freshly cleaned cremini mushrooms.

1. Preheat your oven to 375 degrees F

2. In a bowl, whisk together the butter, thyme, garlic, and vinegar

3. Spread your mushroom into an even layer on a baking sheet and pour the butter mixture above over them

4. Season your dish with kosher salt and pepper according to your preferences

5. Roast your mushrooms in the oven for about 15 to 18 minutes or until they turn golden brown and tender.

With that, you have your cremini mushroom cooked in garlic butter. This dish is quite delicious and can be served at any time of the day. The beauty of it all is that it takes just 15 minutes to get ready.

PORTOBELLO MUSHROOM

Portobello mushroom is a basidiomycete species of mushroom, which is among the edible types of mushrooms. This type of mushroom is native to Europe and North America, even though it grows in other parts of the world. The portobello mushroom has two-color states while immature - white and brown- and takes a dark brownish color while mature.

Characteristics: The portobello mushroom is identified by its smooth caps that range from light brown to dark brown and even tan. The mushroom is firm and thick, with a spongy underneath. It has a small ring with a fibrous stem. The stem itself is quite dense and pure white in color.

Edible Parts: Unlike other types of mushrooms where the stem and the cap are edible, the portobello can be quite cumbersome if you choose to eat the stem. Due to its thick fiber, most people prefer to discard the stem and only consume the cap. Even so, you may still choose to consume the stem if you are okay with its thick fiber.

Environment Where Found: The portobello is native to Europe and North America but can grow in other parts. Generally, the mushroom thrives in compost. In other words, it grows in naturally decaying organic matter. The mushroom needs sufficient moisture and some sunshine. In the U.S, it thrives on the western coast and central states.

Taste profile: The portobello mushroom is similar to cremini in taste. It has an earthy taste but with a meaty flavor. If you have used cremini or button mushrooms, you should easily relate to their taste. The beauty of portobello is that its taste is intense and quite fulfilling as compared to other mushrooms.

Harvesting and usage: The ideal time to harvest the portobello mushroom is during the early morning hours. The mushrooms are mature and ready for harvesting just before the edges of the caps turn flat. To harvest, you will have to dig the mushrooms out of the compost with your hands.

Recipe: Baked Portobello Mushrooms

Just as is the case with other types of mushrooms, the portobello mushroom can be cooked in many ways. Ranging from frying and grilling to boiling and baking, these mushrooms have more to offer to foragers.

340g of portobello mushrooms

1 clove of garlic

2 tablespoons of olive oil

some salt and pepper

½ teaspoon of dried thyme

½ tablespoon of butter

1 tablespoon of grated parmesan

3 tablespoons of mozzarella

1. Preheat your oven to about 400°F/200C.

2. Wipe your mushrooms clean, then remove the stems. Chop and mince all the mushrooms.

3. Oil a baking sheet and arrange your mushrooms in a single layer.

4. In a bowl, mix the oil, garlic, thyme, and little salt. Divide the mixture between your mushrooms and sprinkle some on the inside of the mushrooms.

5. Bake your mushrooms for about 15 minutes or until they turn tender

6. While your mushrooms are still cooking, mix them with cheese. Let them bake for about 15 minutes, then top your mushrooms with cheese and place in the oven for about 5 minutes.

With that, you have your baked portobello mushrooms ready for serving. The dish is delicious and is made in the same manner as other types of edible mushrooms.

Flowers and Fruits

As with mushrooms, flowers and fruits also come in all manner of shapes and sizes. Of the more than 400,000 species of plants on our planet, about half of these are deemed edible for human consumption. But we humans are picky eaters, or rather our ancestors are since we only eat around 200 of these species.

These 200 species that we regularly ingest are what we call domesticated plants chosen because they are easier to propagate. These plants were pruned and perfected through centuries of selection and farming. What we have now in our farms and orchards is a far cry from their early ancestors in terms of taste, nutritional value, and appearance. But that is not to say that the other undomesticated plants - or wild plants as we call them - are not palatable or good for you.

A walk through the wild with an open mind can lead you to a more adventurous and, at the same time, more sustainable diet. You can discover plants that you didn't know about and wild versions of the cultivated ones you are familiar with.

SASKATOON

Saskatoon (*Amelanchier alnifolia*) is a shrub from the Rose (*Rosaceae*) family, which got its name from the Cree word "misâskwatômina," meaning the fruit of the tree with many branches.

A large and deciduous shrub that produces edible fruits that are similar to berries, it is native to the northern parts of the US, the western parts of Canada, and Alaska. It is known by many names depending on where you are: Pacific serviceberry, dwarf shadbush, prairie berry, and juneberry.

Characteristics: The saskatoon shrub only grows up to 1 - 8 meters tall. It rarely grows any bigger than 10 meters and can have a width of about 3 meters. The shrub's growth can occasionally grow to form colonies or sometimes appear clumped together. The trunk is smooth and grey. When young, it will show dark-colored stripes that will roughen and develop longer furrows as it gets older.

The branches swoop upwards in a way that looks like it is parallel to the main trunk. Younger twigs are hairy; these will smoothen as the shrub matures. In winter, the branches are colored reddish-brown with red-purple leaf buds.

Rabbits, deer, elk, and other livestock feed on deciduous leaves that can span from 3 to 6 cm long and 1 - 4.5 cm wide. These are oval or oblong - nearly circular - in shape, with fine-toothed edges and a rounded base. The apex or the tip of the leaves are rounded with a pointed projection. When young, the leaves will be textured with fine, short, and soft hairs that will gradually smoothen and achieve a darker green hue as it matures.

Depending on the location, saskatoon shrubs will produce white flowers from late April to June and will have fruits that will ripen around late June to early July. For places nearer to the coast, the fruits will ripen as summer starts and later in the summer as we go further inland. The flowers have a cluster of 5 oblong or lance-shaped petals that are a little bit spaced out from each other, with individual petals measuring 8 to 10 cm in diameter.

The fruits, at first glance, can look similar to wild blueberries in color, shape, and size - the berries are around 1.5 cm in diameter - but the shrub is more closely related to the apple family. Like apples, saskatoon berries will continue to ripen even after it is picked and when cut open; the cores will look very similar to the ones you would find in apples and pears and will have around 2 to 5 seeds. Squirrels, birds, bears, and other wildlife feed on these berries.

Environment: Saskatoon shrubs can be found in woods, thickets, swamps along roadsides, streams, and hillsides. The shrub is not picky when it comes to soil conditions, but they will tend to grow a lot better in sandy loam and will struggle when the soil has a lot more clay in it or is badly drained. They also prefer soils that have a pH value between 5.5 to 7.0 but can still otherwise do well in a broader pH spectrum. Aside from Canada and the US, from which the shrub is native, the saskatoon also grows in some parts of Europe.

Edible parts: There are a few different species of the saskatoon shrub, with Amelanchier Canadensis being the more popular one in the US and in the eastern part of Canada. When fully ripened, the berries are sweet with a full-bodied fruit flavor. High in fiber, protein, antioxidants, and many other nutrients, these berries are considered a popular annual treat and are cultivated in the northern part of the US and Europe.

Recipe: Saskatoon and Sweet Pear Cake

Batter ingredients:

Half a cup of saskatoon berries (diced or mashed)

⅓ cup of sweet pears (diced or mashed)

2 large eggs

A cup of milk

2 ⅔ of all-purpose flour

2 tsp of baking powder

½ cup of sugar

⅔ cup of butter

Salt

Icing ingredients:

¼ cup of saskatoon berries (diced or mashed)

¼ cup of sweet pears (diced or mashed)

3 cups of icing sugar

⅓ cup of butter (soften to room temperature)

1 tbsp of milk

1. Grease two cake tins (8 inches) and line them with baking or parchment paper. Preheat the oven to 350° F.

2. To make the batter, place half of the diced sweet pears and saskatoon berries together with the eggs and butter. Mix well until fully combined, then add the milk and mix thoroughly.

3. Sift the all-purpose flour and the baking powder together to remove lumps. Add in the sugar and salt. Gently fold the dry

ingredients into the liquid batter slowly until the batter is well combined. Then add the remaining diced saskatoon berries and sweet pears; fold these gently into the batter. If you are using diced saskatoon berries and sweet pears, a few swirls with your spatula should do it. You want a cake that contains visible bits and pieces of the fruits when you slice into it. However, if you prefer a cake with a smoother texture, use mashed fruits and mix this into the batter thoroughly.

4. Pour the batter onto the cake pans. Give the bottom of the pan a couple of taps on the counter to displace the larger air bubbles, then place them inside the preheated oven. Set the timer for 30 to 35 minutes.

5. To check if the cake is done, insert a wooden toothpick right in the middle. It's cooked through when the toothpick comes out clean without any uncooked batter sticking to it. When done baking, place it on top of a cooling rack.

6. While you are waiting for the cakes to cool down, prepare the icing.

7. In a bowl, mix the icing sugar and the softened butter together. Mix thoroughly while pressing on the butter to break it apart, then add the milk. When everything is combined, add in the diced saskatoon berries and sweet pears. Adjust the icing consistency to your liking. For thicker icing, add more icing sugar. If you would like a runnier icing, add more milk.

LAVENDER

Lavender (*Lavendula*) is an all-around herb used from perfumery to cooking. Unbeknownst to most people, lavender can be eaten if it is grown without pesticides and when not treated with chemicals and preservatives. Sadly, most of the lavender we use and see in stores is not culinary grade lavender, so it would be unwise to just go to the town florist and buy a bunch of lavender for cooking. Culinary lavender - as the chefs call it - is lavender that has been subject to food and safety regulations. Specialty stores online and offline might be able to sell you culinary lavender, but it is possible to find wild lavender growing in patches in the wild.

Characteristics: Lavender belongs to the flowering plants in the mint family. The lavender genus itself has many varieties and includes short-lived herbaceous perennial plants, small shrubs, and shrub-like perennials. The plants are small shrubs that spread or branch out with grey-green leaves with purple to blue flowers. The whole plant, from the stem to the top of the flowers, can grow to heights of 0.4 meters in height and can live for 20 to 30 years.

The leaf shape varies across the entire genus. They can be simple in the more commonly cultivated species, with other varieties having leaves with shapes that can range from pinnate to dissected and multiple pinnate. Most leaves in the genus, however, will have

41

fine hairs covering the leaves and will measure around 20 to 50 mm in length

The flowers come in hues that can differ from lilac to blue in the lavenders you can find in the wild. These grow in whorls, radiating from a single point on the stem and wrapping around it with spikes holding it to rise above the foliage.

Environment: The plant is native to Afro-Eurasia, or what is better known as the old world, but can also be found cultivated or growing wild in the temperate zone in the US and Canada. As such, it can grow well in a large range of climates - but optimal temperatures are between 44.6° to 69.8 °F.

The plants will require sunlight and good air circulation but can be grown and kept in a pot indoors. It will flourish in dry, well-draining soils that are a bit sandy or gravelly and have a pH level of 5.8 to 8.3. It will need no fertilizer as well. To ensure a healthy lavender plant, harvest the flowers promptly and remove faded blooms regularly.

As you can see, it is relatively easy to cultivate a lavender plant in the comfort of your own home. Although it will require you to water it regularly while it is still young, it will be drought tolerant when it matures and will require less maintenance. In fact, the infamous lavender patch we have behind the manor on the hillside does not need tending. It just grows in wild abandon there.

Because of this hardiness, even with all of lavender's lauded medicinal uses, lavender can be seen as invasive when it grows wild and spontaneous. It is considered a weed in some parts of Spain. While in Australia, the species *Lavandula stoechas* has been considered a noxious weed in Victoria since 1920.

Edible parts: For the most part, the English lavender is widely considered as the most commonly used lavender when it comes to culinary purposes. But lavender that is grown organically or harvested in the wild can also be treated as an herb for cooking. Herbalists would say that all of the parts of the lavender plant can be used, but the most popular part would be the buds or the flowers themselves.

Lavender has a sweet fragrance and has a small hint of citrus in it. The fresh flowers can be used as a flavoring to food and pastry. It is most commonly added to pasta and salad dressings. Dried buds can be used as an herb, while the fresh greens have a more subtle taste when compared to rosemary.

Like most, drying lavender flowers will amplify the taste of the flowers; too much dried lavender will yield a soapy aftertaste. Recipes that call for fresh lavender flowers should be adjusted accordingly if you plan to use dried flowers instead. I would suggest a third of the number of fresh flowers. Meanwhile, the buds and greens can be used for teas, with the leaves lending the tea a more subtle fragrance and taste.

The buds also contain a higher amount of nectar, so honey collected from bees that use lavender flowers is marketed as monofloral honey and is considered high-quality products.

Lavender essential oils, extracted by steam distillation, are said to have a number of medical properties, although these claims lack our modern-day clinical studies. The purported healing properties of lavender can be traced back centuries in human history through the ancient lands of Iraq, Greece, and Rome. Herbalists laud the medical effects of lavender. It is said to help with insomnia, stress, and anxiety, as it acts like a gentle sedative. It is also anti-inflammatory, so lavender balms and salves are used to treat minor wounds as well as sores, toothaches, headaches, and sprains.

Today, the lavender plant is grown commercially for its essential oil. The English lavender is counted as the most popular species as it produces an oil that has sweet overtones. This oil is mainly used for balms, perfumes, salves, and other cosmetic uses.

Hybrid lavender also exists and produces a bigger flower head that's easier to harvest and can yield a larger amount of essential oil. But the oil extracted from these hybrids is subpar when compared to oils extracted from the English lavender.

Aside from their culinary uses, dried lavender flowers, because of their fragrance, are used as potpourris. You can find cloth sachets of lavender sold in organic markets for freshening and moth-proofing your linens and clothes. Recently, it has also become a popular alternative to tobacco as a smoking herb.

Recipe: Lavender Cookies

5 to 6 teaspoons of fresh lavender flowers or 2 teaspoons of dried lavender

1 cup of sugar

1 teaspoon of vanilla extract

1 ½ cup of softened butter

3 cups of all-purpose flour

Salt

1. If you are using fresh lavender flowers, finely chop them into little pieces or use a food processor. Dried lavender, on the other

hand, should be ground to powder. You can also use a food processor, or you may choose to use a stone or marble mortar and pestle.

2. In a bowl, mix all the dry ingredients - flour, sugar and salt, along with the lavender (dry or not) - together. Add the softened butter and mash it into the dry mixture until you can form a dough.

3. Next, add in the vanilla extract and knead until the extract is fully mixed. Take the dough out of the bowl. Do not forget to scrape the sides of the bowl and flatten it to around half an inch thick with a rolling pin onto a baking sheet.

4. Grab your cookie cutters and press them gently into the dough. Place the cookie dough into a separate sheet of baking paper that you will place in the fridge to cool for an hour.

5. While the cookie dough is in the fridge, preheat the oven to 350° F. After an hour, take the cookie dough out of the fridge. These should be firm to touch. Set the timer to 20 to 25 minutes and bake the cookies in the oven. The cookies should come out with light golden brown edges. Transfer the cookies carefully onto a drying rack and let it cool. You can choose to dust it with powdered sugar or lavender sugar. Serve.

ELDERBERRY

Elderberry (*Sambucus*) is a genus of the flowering plants in the *moschatel* family or Adoxaceae. If you have an older field guide, it used to be classified under the honeysuckle family (*Caprifoliaceae*). Through the years, it was mostly propagated as an ornamental shrub, but most recently, it gained popularity as a dietary supplement. It is now easy to find *Sambucus* extracts claiming to treat constipation, flu, or colds in the local pharmacies.

In popular culture, folklore would often associate the elder trees with witches and certain pagan traditions. A wand made from the branch of an elder tree even made an appearance in the popular book series "Harry Potter."

Characteristics: The elderberry plant has a short trunk that is covered with smooth and gray-brown bark. It is covered with cork-like bumps and a furrowed bark. The bark of the more mature plants has a brown-gray color accentuated with shallower fissures as it becomes rougher with time by the development of scales that are thin and plate-like.

The plant can reach about 3 meters in height and can grow as wide as it is tall. Twigs are hairless, and pinnate leaves at 5 to 9 leaflets are arranged opposite each other, with each leaf measured at 5 to 30 cm in length. It is dark green and has serrated edges.

It will bear large clusters of small flowers that are 15 to 30 cm in diameter and are cream-colored to white. The 5 petals are radially symmetrical, flat, and umbrella-shaped. Each flower will also have 5 stamens that are protruding.

The flowers will turn into drooping clusters of fruits or berries that are edible and colored a deep purple-black to black. Each individual fruit measures 3 to 5 cm in diameter and will ripen around the middle of August to September.

Environment: Growing in the temperate and subtropical zones, this plant is widespread in the northern parts of the US, the east of the Rocky Mountains, and can grow wild in parts of Mexico and Central America. It can be found growing near organic wastes as it is nitrogen dependent; thus, you can find it growing wild near homesteads and farms. In England, due to its characteristic to grow fast and profusely, it is known as "instant hedge" as it can be bent into any shape and is, therefore, the best for building hedges.

It will grow on any soil type or in any pH level - but it will thrive in moist soil and would only require sufficient sunlight.

Edible parts: The fruits and the flowers of most species of this plant are edible. You can find fresh elderberry flowers used in salads with the berries regularly used in pies, jams, and wine. However, for some species, uncooked berries and other parts of this plant are poisonous as it contains calcium oxalate crystals that are considered toxic. Elderberries are found to contain anthocyanins that are usually used in cough syrups.

Recipe: Flake-y Elderberry Meringue Pie

Pie crust:

2 and a half cups of all-purpose flour

6 tablespoons or ⅓ cup of butter (cubed)

¾ cup of vegetable shortening

Salt

Half a cup of ice water

Elderberry filling:

1 and a half cups of fresh elderberries

1 cup of sugar

Salt

Half a cup of water

4 eggs yolks

2 tablespoons of melted butter

Meringue:

Half a cup of lemon juice

Half a teaspoon of vanilla extract

Half a cup of sugar

4 egg whites

1. In a mixing bowl, mix the dry ingredients together: flour and salt. When fully mixed, add the butter and vegetable shortening. The butter should be cold when it is added in, so it is better to cut it up into cubes. You can choose to use a fork or a pastry knife to blend the butter and the vegetable shortening into the dough. The resulting dough should look crumbly. It is fine if you have larger pea-sized pieces of butter clumping up.

2. Mix it with a rubber spatula as you add the iced or cold water a tablespoon at a time to the dough until the dough starts to form larger clumps.

3. Flour your work surface and your hands and work the dough. Flatten it into a disk that is around 1 inch thick. Wrap it in plastic wrap and refrigerate for 2 hours or overnight.

4. After the pie dough has been adequately chilled in the fridge, take it out and gently roll it flat with a rolling pin. Always start from the center and roll outwards, turning slightly as you go along. Gently lay this on your pie pan. Leave around 1 to 2 cm doping from the edge of the pan and cut the rest off.

5. Preheat the oven at 350º F. While the oven is preheating, prepare the elderberry juice. Bring the elderberries to a boil with 1

cup of water. Let it simmer for 10 minutes, then take it off the heat. While still hot, mash the berries. Set a strainer over a bowl and cover it with a cheesecloth. Pour the mashed elderberries onto the cheesecloth and then strain. Set it aside to let it cool first before proceeding to the next step.

6. In a saucepan, add the sugar, flour, salt, and elderberry juice together. Cook it in medium heat while whisking constantly until the mixture has thickened enough to a smooth custard-like consistency.

7. In another bowl, beat the egg yolks together and add half of the elderberry mixture into the eggs slowly, careful not to cook the yolk. When thoroughly mixed, add this egg mixture back into the remaining elderberry mixture and whisk it again. Heat the mixture again while whisking constantly. Add the butter and the lemon juice and whisk until everything is smooth. Pour the mixture into the dough-covered pie pan.

8. To make the meringue, beat the egg whites in a stand mixer on high and add in the vanilla extracts and cream of tartar. Slowly add the sugar in 3 stages until it forms stiff peaks. Scoop the meringue out and gently spread over the elderberry mixture.

9. Place the pie into the oven and bake it for 10 to 15 minutes or until the meringue tips are golden brown. Let it rest on a cooling rack before serving.

WILD STRAWBERRY

Wild strawberry (*Fragaria virginiana*) is also known as Virginia strawberry, mountain strawberry, and common strawberry. Part of the rose (*Rosaceae*) family, this herbaceous perennial is abundant in North America and across the southern part of Canada. It is a runner. It grows low and close to the ground, with the roots turning into new plants eventually. This species is the parent of the common garden strawberry (*Fragaria × ananassa*) - the modern domesticated version that we see in markets today - as it is a hybrid version of two wild strawberries.

Characteristics: Wild strawberries only grow up to 100 mm tall. They grow horizontally, hugging the ground, so it might be harder to find them in the wild, especially if they are surrounded by taller plants. It grows trifoliate leaves that are measured at around 40 mm in width and 75 mm in length. These are pale green when they are low on the ground and turn green as they grow nearer to the top. Attached to hairy stems, each leaf is oval in shape with toothed or serrated edges all the way to the apex except for the base, which is relatively smooth. The surface is matte, with short silky hairs on the underside.

The white flowers are measured at 7 to 10 cm in diameter and bloom around April to May. They grow in clusters with 5 petals on each and numerous pistils nestled between yellow stamens that are typical of the rose family. Under the flowers are 10 smaller sepals. The bright red aggregate fruits - or berries - of the wild strawberry will ripen around June to July and are measured at around 1.25 cm or an inch in diameter. Much smaller than that of the common garden strawberry, they are round and heart-shaped, with the seeds visible and sunken into the skin of the fruit.

Environment: These are native to North America and have been growing here before Columbus discovered the land. They can be found growing unexpectedly in yards, gardens, on roadsides, in abandoned fields, along railroad tracks, and often near woodlands during the early spring to deep in the summer months. The plant thrives under the sun and on moist, fertile soil that contains loam.

Considered a cool-season plant, it can grow wildly in colonies during the spring and autumn months and dormant during the hot summer months after it bears fruit. It is also relatively easy to cultivate, with flowers blooming regularly during spring. But weather conditions will dictate in the end if the plant will bear fruit during the summer months. Watering them during spring when the flowers are blooming may help push the plants to bear fruits.

Otherwise, it will spread and cover open areas with relative ease. This ease and speed with which it grows is also the reason why some species, especially mock strawberries that are native to South Asia, are considered as invasive. Wild strawberries that also grow out of hand in yards and untended gardens are also sometimes considered a nuisance.

Edible parts: The fruits are edible and are considered to be the miniature version of the common garden strawberries. It has a sweet and tart flavor.

The leaves are also edible and can be used raw and cooked. Although the grassy and slightly astringent finish of the fresh leaves may put off some people, it still has a mild fruity flavor to it that makes it a good and popular addition to salads. It is a good source of antioxidants, vitamins C, K, and tannin and is purported to be able to boost the immune system.

Before, crushed leaves were used by the Native Americans on burns and sores due to their antiseptic and disinfectant properties.

Recipe: Wild Strawberry-infused Vinegar

3 cups of fresh wild strawberries

5 tablespoons of sugar (honey or maple syrup are also good alternatives)

A quarter of a cup of cognac or brandy

2 cups of white wine vinegar (choose to use high-quality vinegar for this recipe)

1. To prepare the infusion, first, divide the strawberries into equal halves. Place the first half into a container and store it in the fridge for later. The 2nd half should be placed in a large enough mason jar. Pour in the white wine vinegar, sugar or maple syrup, and alcohol on top of the strawberries. Place the cover back on and allow the mixture to steep for 48 hours while stirring occasionally after every few hours. When you stir, gently press on the strawberries to break them apart but not enough to mash them.

2. After 48 hours, take the strawberries out of the vinegar mixture and drain well. Do not throw these away, as these can be repurposed to make jams and pies afterward. Repeat the infusion steps for the second time by replacing the strawberries with the first half you have stored in your fridge. Let it sit for 48 hours and again stir occasionally while breaking apart the strawberries.

3. After the second 48 hours, take the strawberries and drain them well. You will then need to transfer the strawberry vinegar mixture into a bowl that is placed over simmering water. Let the mixture slowly heat up for about 30 minutes.

4. When 30 minutes have passed, take the bowl off the simmering water and let it stand to room temperature before bottling and storing. Combining this vinegar infusion with a good hazelnut oil will make for a great salad dressing.

Recipe: Wild Strawberry Leaf Tea

Freshly harvested strawberry leaves

Strawberry leaf tea is relatively easy to make. You can make it with either fresh or dried wild strawberry leaves. When harvesting the leaves, choose a whole clean leaf without any signs of bug infestation or fungi, then wash the leaves quickly and carefully under running water.

For the fresh ones, just drop a leaf into your tea cup and bring water to a boil. Let the water sit for a few seconds after it boils, then pour this over the leaf. You may choose to add sweeteners.

To dry strawberry leaves for future tea brewing, you can opt to use a dehydrator or just simply use the power of the sun. Lay the leaves out flat on a large tray and leave it out under the sun until it has become dry. Collect and store this in an airtight container.

AUTUMN OLIVE

Autumn Olive (*Elaeagnus umbellata*), otherwise known as the Japanese Silverberry, is a medium to a large deciduous shrub that is native to Asia. It was brought into the New World during the 1930s as an ornamental plant as well as providing food and shelter for the local wildlife. It is also planted along roads and on ridges by the Soil Conservation Service as erosion control. Sadly, it is now considered an invasive species as it can grow too fast and too uncontrollably that it displaces other native species.

Characteristics: The autumn olive belongs to the *Elaeagnaceae* family. It is a multi-stemmed shrub that can easily reach heights of 20 feet and 30 feet wide with a dense crown and has spur branches or sharp thorns. The bark is a dry olive color with numerous white lenticels that changes from light grey to greyish brown as it matures. The younger branches have longer thorns and have a silvery sheen to them that is quite distinctive when seen from afar. The brown scales can give it a speckled appearance.

The leaves are alternate and have an oval shape that is measured at 5 to 10 cm in length and 2 to 4 cm in width. It has finely pointed tips with wavy edges that are not toothed. Young leaves are covered with distinct silvery scales as they grow during the early spring months. They take on a darker green hue as the scales drop off when they mature during the summer months, but the undersides of the leaves will retain their silvery scales all throughout.

The small flowers that bloom from April to June are fragrant and grow in clusters of 1 to 8 along the twigs. Their colors can range from cream to light yellow with four tubular petals and stamens. Each individual flower is measured at 7 mm in diameter and 8 to 9 in length. The underside of the petals or the outside of the flowers is also covered in small silvery scales.

Fruits are small, abundant, and fleshy, measured at 5 mm in diameter and 3 to 9 mm in length. They are yellow to brown and also have the distinctive, silvery scale the leaves have. As it ripens, the fruits take on a red hue that is speckled with silver and brown during the months of September to October.

Environment: It is not invasive in Asia, where it is native, but it does grow rapidly over barren wastelands. It requires little to no maintenance and tolerates shade and dry soil but will thrive in loam and clay-based soil and substrates that have a neutral pH of 7.

If cultivated correctly and planted near orchards, its roots - which fixes atmospheric nitrogen - can enrich soils and have been proven to increase the yields of the nearby fruit trees by 10%.

It is easy enough to find autumn olives around the US, especially if you are located in the northeastern or eastern parts. Otherwise, you can get them online from autumnberryinspired.com, a company that farms and sells the nutritious fruits of these trees "by turning this invasive species into a useful commodity." This is a far better idea than to douse the whole tree with chemicals to kill it.

Edible parts: Only the berries are edible and can be eaten raw or cooked. The ripe berries are sweet and tart at the same time and contain carotenoids and a lot of lycopene. It is a popular ingredient in jams and preserves. These shrubs grow a lot of fruits, to the point that the whole tree can sometimes topple over because of it. Harvest the fruits as soon as it turns red. If you are worried about spreading the seeds, cooking and boiling the seeds will stop them from sprouting when thrown out to the compost bin.

Recipe: Autumn Olive Berry Jam

7 and a half cups of autumn olive berries

2 cups of sugar

3 teaspoons of unflavored gelatin, but you can choose to use 2 under-ripe apples, unpeeled for pectin instead

1 and a half tablespoons of lemon juice

3 cups of water

1. Pectin is a gelling agent similar to gelatin. Gelatin usually comes from animals, while pectin comes from fruits and vegetables. If you are using apples for pectin, take the cores out and chop them up, then place the apples, the autumn olive berries, and water into a saucepan. Let it simmer for 15 minutes in medium heat while stirring constantly. Gently mash the apples and berries while you stir.

2. Place a fine-meshed strainer over a big bowl and pour the mixture in. Push the pulp through the strainer but be careful not to let the skins and the seeds through. Place this strained mixture back into your saucepan and add in the sugar and lemon juice. If you are using gelatin instead of pectin, now is the right time to add it in.

Whisk the gelatin in until thoroughly melted and incorporated into the mixture.

3. Then, let the mixture come back into a simmer once again while stirring constantly. Remember to scrape the bottom of your pan with your spatula to keep it from scorching.

4. When you see the mixture falling off in sheets from your spoon, take it off the heat. It will get thicker before it gels. Pour the mixture into sterilized mason jars. If you want them to keep for longer, you can do canning with the jars the old-fashioned way.

5. After closing the jars, place them in a boiling water bath for 15 minutes - with water covering the tops of the jar lids. Keep the water boiling for 15 minutes; do not turn the heat down. After 15 minutes, take the jars out of the boiling water and let them stand to room temperature. The resulting jam will be able to keep for months on a cool and dry shelf.

DANDELIONS

Dandelions are among the most popular flowers across the US. The fact that the yellow flowers can grow naturally in most areas makes them a good option for those looking or forging plants. Scientifically known as Taraxacum, the flower belongs to the Asteraceae family, which contains many flowers that are commonly referred to as dandelions.

These flowers are rich in vitamins and minerals, making them very popular among foragers. Some experts say that they are more nutritious than kale and spinach. They are a known source for vitamins A, C, and K.

Characteristics: The dandelion plant itself is a taproot. This consequently means that it can grow in many parts, even in an area where water access is a problem. Its roots grow up to 6 inches, helping the plant to fetch water from deep soil profiles. This also makes it difficult to extract when it is time to harvest.

At an early age, the leaves grow from the base of the plant. As it matures, the leaves develop in the stem, which holds all the other leaves. The stem can grow all the way to 24 inches. However, in most cases, the stems do not grow past 6 o 7 inches.

The flowers show up on the stems in spring in most parts of the US. The flowers are bright yellow and can be harvested alongside other parts of the plant. With the dandelion, the beauty and use of the plant are limitless.

Edible Parts: Ideally, every part of the dandelion plant is edible. Its roots, stems, leaves, and flowers can be eaten in different ways. These parts also serve different purposes ranging from medicinal to nutritional uses. The leaves, for instance, are purely taken for their nutrition. They are a rich source of vitamins, as mentioned but are also a source of carotene, fiber, potassium, and iron. The roots are rich in calcium, phosphorous, and iron. The roots, on the other hand, are rich sources of vitamin B and protein.

Environment Where they Grow: The dandelion flower is one of the most resilient plants of this era. This flower can grow virtually anywhere. In the US, it is known to grow from coast to coast. It does not choose soil profile or climatic condition as is the case with other plants. We have spotted this plant at the manor and other places across the country as we travel

Some of the storage places I have seen the dandelions include wetlands and forests. The flower can be planted in lawns, fields, and gardens. If you will be using your dandelion for food, do not use artificial pesticides on it. This will mean that you have to grow it away from other garden plants that may require regular spraying.

Taste Profile: The dandelion is not a sweet plat that you may enjoy eating. Most parts, including the roots and the leaves, are slightly bitter. The flowers and leaves have a tangy flavor that is similar to spinach. The flowers are loved for their sweet scent. They are commonly used to infuse honey and vinegar as well as other drinks at home.

Harvesting and Usage: All parts of the dandelion are legible for use and can be harvested. Even so, always remember the rules of foraging we have discussed in previous chapters. Overharvesting any species may lead to depletion and, in some cases, extinction.

The ideal way to harvest dandelions is to uproot the entire plant. This way, you get to choose which part you wish to use. However, if you are quite sure you will not be using the roots or the stem, stick to harvesting the flowers and the leaves. This way, you leave the root and the stem to produce further.

The ideal time to harvest dandelions is in the morning hours. Morning time works best for most plants that must be used while still fresh. However, make sure you do not harvest plants that have been sprayed with herbicides. Only harvest naturally growing dandelions that have not been contaminated by pollution.

Recipe: Sauteed Dandelion Greens with Eggs

If you are new to dandelions and do not know how to use them, consider the following recipe. Even so, there are plenty of other recipes you must try to enjoy the benefits that the plant has to offer.

Sauteed dandelions taste more like spinach. They can be prepared in a similar way, but for this recipe, we will mix our dandelions with eggs.

4 cups of chopped dandelion greens

2 tablespoons of butter- unsalted clarified.

1 large leek finely chopped lengthwise

4 large eggs

1/ cup of crumbled feta cheese

1. Boil a large pot of water and add some salt to it. Add your chopped dandelions and blanch for about 2 minutes.

2. Drain the greens using a wooden spoon, pressing to release as much water as possible.

3. Melt your butter in a 10-inch sauté over medium heat. Sauté your leeks until they are tender or for about 5 minutes. Once they are tender, add the drained dandelions, one spoonful at a time.

4. Once your greens are wilted, use a spoon to create several shallow nests in your greens and crack your eggs into each one.

5. Top up with feta cheese and cook while uncovered until the whites of the eggs are well set.

6. Serve your food immediately with toasted slices of crusty bread.

We love this recipe with family; it is one of the easy foods we can repair even when we are not in the mood. Ideally, the recipe takes about 38 minutes to be ready.

BLACKBERRIES

Blackberries have been hailed as superfoods due to their rich nutritional profile. The fruit is very sweet and one of the favorites in most American homes. Blackberries are produced by many species in the genus *Rubus* in the family *Rosaceae*. However, most farmers opt for hybrids within this family in the subgenus *Rubus*.

Foraging berries can be quite satisfying for various reasons. The fruits are hard to come by, but when you find some, they are very sweet. Secondly, you can eat the fruits on the spot thanks to their rich flavor profile.

Characteristics: There are different types of berries that can be classified as blackberries, as already highlighted above. The way a tree looks depends on the species. The common berries types are either trailing, erect or semi-trailing. There are also some species that are thorny while others are thornless. If you will be foraging on thorny berries, you must be careful not to hurt yourself.

With most blackberries species, the tree spreads between 10 and 20 feet. We have a few berries on our farm that are about 14 to 15 feet wide. In our first year of planting, the berry bark spread past 6 feet. By the second year, the berry has spread about 15 feet.

Edible Parts: Like is the case with most fruiting plants, the fruits of blackberries are the priority among foragers. Even so, you may be surprised to realize that other parts of the plant are also very useful. For instance, the root and leaves are well-known medical compounds. The shrub is also used to attract wildlife.

The parts that can be eaten raw on blackberry plants are the young leaves, the young ground shot, and fruits. The fruit is the most popular among all the edible parts and also the sweetest.

Environment where Found: Blackberries are native to Europe, Asia, South America and parts of North America. The fruit thrives in warm climates such as South America and the tropical regions of Asia. However, it also needs cool nights to survive. Ideally, blackberries must be planted in regions with about 6 to 8 hours of sunshine and a cool night.

For those looking to plant or domesticate blackberries, consider your location and local climate. The fruit will thrive in southern states such as North and South Carolina and Louisiana.

Taste profile: The taste of the back berry is one of the richest among fruits. In taste, they are almost similar to grapes. Even so, domestic blackberries can be quite bitter or sour. The taste varies depending on how well ripped the fruit is when harvested. The sweetest are those that are well-ripened when harvested, hence the saying "the darker the berry, the sweeter the juice."

Harvesting and usage: Grapes, just like scuppernongs, are only harvested when they are ripe. With berries, they must be used immediately after harvesting since they can go bad in a few days or even hours.

To harvest berries, pick a time of the day when the fields are cool such as early morning or evening. Do not pick berries during the day when the sun is overhead since this can lead to weathering of the fruits.

You are only required to pick berries that are fully ripe; in this case, only pick those that are black in color. It is also important to note that you should only pick the ones you can use. If you pick excess berries, you may end up wasting them unless you refrigerate them.

Once berries start ripping, they should be picked either daily or every two days. This is because the plant produces plenty of fruits that get ripe in close successions. When you pick your berries, keep the central plug within the fruit to avoid contamination. For mass harvesting, you may shake the tree and pick the ready fruits on the ground. Although this approach is not encouraged.

Recipe: Blackberry Cobbler Recipe

There are many recipes you could choose to make when dealing with blackberries. You may either take the fruits raw or use them to garnish your cakes and other meals. The most common recipe is preparing a blackberry. However, for this book, I will show you a special recipe I learned while in the manor from a guest from the south.

4 cups of fresh blackberries

1 tablespoon of lemon juice

1 large egg

1 cup of sugar

1 cup of all-purpose flour

6 tablespoons of melted butter

Optional whipped cream

1. Preheat your oven to about 370 degrees F

2. Place your blackberries in a lightly greased 8-inch square baking dish and sprinkle them with some lemon juice.

3. In a different saucepan, break the egg and beat it well.

4. Add your flour and sugar to a larger saucepan and mix well with your hand. Add in the beaten egg above and mix well with your hand until the mixture resembles a coarse meal.

5. Sprinkle the flour mixture above your fruits and drizzle the melted butter over it.

6. Bake the contents in your can in the oven for about 35 degrees C or until they are lightly browned.

7. Remove your dish from the oven and let it stand for about 10 minutes before serving. You may garnish with some fresh blackberries or a fresh mint sprig if you wish.

8. If you wish to have a much neater presentation for your meal, you may bake for the same time in 6-ounce ramekins on aluminum foil.

This is one of the easiest recipes to prepare for those who do not know what to do with their blackberries. It is important to remember that this recipe can only be achieved if you are in a location where you can bake. If you are out in the fields like most foragers, avoid baking entirely and opt for simple none bake recipes. One of the easy non-bake recipes is one that involves the making of jelly or jam. You can use berries in the same way as we used the scuppernong in the recipe above to come up with a sweet berry jam.

Do not use all berries in a similar manner. Blackberries are very different from strawberries and raspberries. When foraging, make sure you pick each fruit at the right time and in the right manner. To prevent the confusion I had when I started foraging, I am going to give you a bit more information about raspberries below. They're quite different from blackberries.

RASPBERRIES

Raspberries are also very popular across the US. They can easily be purchased from local grocery stores at an affordable price. However, store-bought fruits are just a shadow of what the real wild fruits taste like. If you are into foraging and wish to enjoy the raw natural taste of wild raspberries, then you should try finding some. There are many locations where you can find these fruits occurring naturally. Due to my love for berries, I have planted a few trees just to enjoy their natural flavor.

All raspberries are self-fertile, so you do not need to grow several trees to get the producing fruits. They can get pollinated by bees and start producing one year from planting time. These plants are inclined to grow in cooler regions but are now found even in warmer states thanks to modern hybrid species.

Characteristics: The raspberry plant grows approximately 4 to 6 feet high, but some species are much shorter. The plant has a woody rounded and erect red stem usually fitted with overhand branches. Some species have thorns on their branches, while some are plain with tiny green leaves.

The raspberry plant is much less resistant to diseases and tough weather as compared to blackberries. Even so, the raspberry is not a weak plant. The plant has pinnate leaves with 3 to 7 serrated leaflets. The plant produces flowers when it is about to fruit, with its flower being about 1 cm in diameter.

Edible Parts: Everyone knows that the fruits of raspberries are edible. What most people do not know is that the roots and leaves are also edible. The roots and leaves are particularly loved for their medicinal value. The leaves can be eaten raw, but they are bitter; hence they are commonly used to prepare tea. Their tea has some medicinal components in terms of boosting digestion and cleansing the body.

Environment where found: You can only forage a plant that is available in your locality. If you are after raspberries, you must know that they rarely grow in the wild. They grow naturally in cooler regions, especially in the coastal areas. In America, they are well adapted to the cool coastal climate of the western US, especially California.

Given that the fruits require full sun to grow to maturity, you may not be able to come across the fruits if you live far north. With that said, there are some species that have been found to do well when cultivated in other regions. For instance, the Bababerry and Oregon 1030 are well tolerant to heat and are grown in the southern valleys of California. Some have even been grown in southern states, especially Georgia.

For those who live in warmer regions and wish to grow raspberries, it is advisable to use shade. We have some raspberries on our farm, although they are under pine trees. This is a trick you may use if you wish to plant the fruit in warmer regions. However, one must also remember that the fruit needs full sun, so do not grow it under a shade that will completely prevent sun rays from reaching the tree.

Taste profile: The taste of raspberries is slightly different from that of blackberries. While blackberries are sweet with some sour, raspberries are mostly sweet. A few raspberries may be tart and sweet, especially those that are harvested before they ripe well. Just as is the case with blackberries, raspberries get sweeter as they are ripe. Those that are harvested when they have attained full ripping are sweeter.

Harvesting and usage: The harvesting of raspberries should be done when they are well ripe. If you harvest unripe berries, they will not get ripe. They may get rotten instead of ripening. The ideal weather to harvest your raspberries is dry and cool. Do not harvest your raspberries early morning since the dew may get you messed up. On the other hand, do not harvest during the midday sun since you may get the fruits to weather.

Experts recommend harvesting on a dry day after the midday sun. I have been involved in harvesting raspberries, and it can be quite fun. At this time, you will enjoy the cool evening breeze as you go about your business. If you fancy eating a few while harvesting, it is all up to you.

Recipe: Raspberry Crumble

Raspberries are among the most regular fruits in modern recipes. Berries are used in many recipes, ranging from fruit salads to juices, smoothies, and even pastry recipes. If you are a fan of raspberries, you have the chance to prepare some amazing dishes with your favorite fruit after foraging. Below is a simple recipe.

Raspberry Filling:

24 ounces of frozen raspberries divided into two equal parts

1/2 a cup of granulated sugar

2 tablespoons of flour

1 tablespoon of cornstarch

1 lemon squeezed.

Crumble Layer:

3 cups of rolled oats

3 cups of flour

2 cups of brown sugar

1 teaspoon of baking powder

2 cups of melted, salted butter

1/2 teaspoon of salt.

1. Preheat your oven to about 350 degrees F and place your berries in a large colander.

2. Run warm water over your berries for about a minute and let all the water drain out in about an hour or so.

3. Mix all your raspberries with sugar, flour, lemon juice, and cornstarch.

4. Once you have prepared your berries, it's time to prepare your crust. Mix all the oats, flour, baking powder, butter, and salt into a bowl with the flour.

5. Work on the ingredients above until they for a crumble like mixture,

6. Press the crumble mixture above into a 9x13 pan lined with parchment paper, leaving behind at least a third of the mixture.

7. Bake the crust in your prepared oven for about 10 minutes.

8. Once your crust is ready, arrange the prepared raspberries on top of the baked bottom layer. Now sprinkle the rest of the crumb-like mixture on top of the berries and bake the two for about 25 minutes.

9. After 25 minutes, remove the berries from the oven and give your cake a little time to chill. You can chill them for about 1 or 2 hours to get them really firm.

10. Once chilled, cut your cake and serve immediately. Some people prefer serving it hot. If that is your case, you do not have to take time to chill

Note: Removing your cake from the pan should not be a problem. You can easily remove it by pulling the parchment paper on the sides of the pan.

With that, you have a good simple recipe you can prepare with raspberries. These fruits are easily accessible for those foraging in the warm western states.

ROSEHIPS

The rosehip plant also referred to as rose hep, is an accessory fruit of the different types of rose plant. Its color generally ranges from red to orange but could vary between dark purple to blackish in some species. It is easy to identify the rose hip plant thanks to its unique color. Keep in mind that rose hip can grow widely, or you can choose to grow it in your garden. Given the many nutritional benefits it comes with, you will find growing rosehip very necessary. It can also be used for culinary purposes, thanks to its unique taste.

Characteristics: Rosehips are unique plants both physically and characteristically. They have roses that could be climbing, erect, or trailing shrubs. Their stems are uniquely armed with prickles of various sizes and shapes. These prickles are commonly referred to as thorns. Given their sharpness, these prickles protect rosehips from danger.

Animals can't feed on them easily, giving them time to grow. Humans are also kept at bay by these thorns. Furthermore, rosehips have leaves that are pinnately compound and alternate. This means their leaves are feather-formed. Besides, they have oval leaflets that are mostly sharply toothed. This is vital because it protects the plant from danger. Rosehips grow to a considerable height, making it easier to harvest them.

Edible Parts: You can eat both rose hips and rose petals. This is because they don't contain any contaminants and are actually good for your health. Rosehips contain the tartness found in crab apples, making them a great source of vitamin C. Keep in mind that this nutrient is very important for your body and helps prevent various conditions.

All the roses on a rosehip plant tend to produce hips through the rugosa roses. The rugosa roses refer to a type of shrub rose species found in most parts of the country. These roses are known to produce the best-tasting hips. Therefore, if you are interested in the tastiest type of rosehip, you should consider those from the rugosa roses. They are also easy to harvest and preserve.

Environment Where Found: The rugosa rose, commonly referred to as the wrinkled rose or large-hip rose, is a plant native to the northern United States and some parts of Canada. You will also find it around sand dunes and the coastal areas. To grow effectively, rosehips require sufficient sunlight and good air circulation.

The coastal areas provide these conditions, making them an ideal location for the rosehip plant. While rosehips grow better in open spaces, you can also grow them indoors. However, you must ensure that it's getting sufficient sunlight to prevent stagnant growth. You also need to water it regularly to avoid drying up.

Taste Profile: The rosehip plant has a delicate, floral flavor that makes it slightly sweet. However, its sweetness comes with a distant tart aftertaste. When used as an ingredient, rosehips can add flavor to your dish. If you likely have slightly sweet dishes but with a distinct aftertaste, you should consider rosehips.

Harvesting and Usage: Rosehips have a wide range of uses. Ideally, the recommended time to harvest your rosehips is after the first light first nipples the leaves. However, you need to avoid exposing them to a hard frost that could freeze the hips. Frozen rosehips are not ideal for consumption and could be tasteless. Therefore, you should harvest your rosehips after a light frost that helps improve the flavor. Before harvesting, you should ensure that the hips are firm and have a good color.

Avoid waiting until the hips are weak and unstable. This could be an indicator that your rosehips are ready for harvest or have grown past the ideal harvesting period. This is why you need to be careful when it comes to harvesting your rosehips. Fully ripe hips have a wide range of uses. For instance, you can consume them directly or use them as ingredients. Given that they are rich in nutrients, rosehips are great additions to various dishes.

Recipe: Rose Hip Tea

1 heaping tbsp. crushed dried rose hips or ¼ cup fresh rose hips

1 tsp. honey (optional)

1. Start by foraging your rosehips. This is important because it prepares them for the next step. It is essential that you forage carefully to avoid removing essential nutrients.

2. Then, boil a pot of water. Keep the temperatures at a medium level to avoid overheating. This step is vital because it helps derive the necessary nutrients from rosehips.

3. Next, pour the hot water over the dried or fresh rosehips. If you are using herbs, you should also pour hot water over them. You should stick to using boiled water because warm or cold water won't get the job done.

4. After that, let the wild rosehip tea steep for around 15 minutes. Ensure that the tea is covered during this period. This prevents bacteria and also helps create an ideal environment for the steeping process. Besides, you should avoid exposing the tea to excessive heat.

5. Then, strain the rosehip tea through a fine mesh filter to get rid of seeds and any other pulp present. This is an important step that helps prepare rosehip tea for consumption. Generally, rosehips have lots of seeds that could find their way into your tea. This is risky, and straining through a fine mesh helps avoid such cases. It also helps keep your rosehip tea smooth and delicious.

6. Lastly, you can sweeten the tea with honey if you desire. You can also choose to consume it without honey. Either way, rosehip tea is tasty and equips your body with essential nutrients.

Notes: It is important to note that the time spent to forage for rosehips is not captured in this recipe. Instead, only the amount of time needed to steep has been captured. You can use either dried or fresh rosehips for your tea!

CHICKWEED

Categorized under the Caryophyllaceae family, chickweed is a perennial and annual flowering plant found in most parts of the country. It is native to Eurasia and naturalized across the world. What most people don't know is that chickweed can be eaten. This is possible if the plant is grown without pesticides and not exposed to chemicals.

Apart from direct consumption, this plant can also be used for culinary purposes. This means you can use it as an ingredient in various dishes. Thanks to its various nutrients, you can find various chickweed products in local supermarkets or online stores.

Characteristics: Chickweed grows about three to eight inches in diameter. The plant forms small mounds in your garden, and it is easy to identify. Mostly, chickweed forms small, daisy-like, delicate, whitish flowers in the spring. They can also form pink flowers depending on the conditions. Keep in mind that these flowers vary in shape and size.

Both the plant's leaves and stem are hairy. This gives the chickweed plant a grayer appearance. It is important to note that the abundance of hairs come with different glandular secretions that give the chickweed plant a sticky feel. This means that when you touch the chickweed plant, you will notice a sticky touch on your fingers. It is also essential to note that both the common and sticky chickweed are annual weeds.

Edible Parts: Even though the chickweed plant is a weed that most farmers find harmful, it is edible. Its leaves and flowers are edible. However, you need to be careful when consuming chickweed. This is because consuming the plant in large quantities can cause stomach upsets. The problem is caused by a large amount of saponins the plant contains. Therefore, it is a good idea to consume chickweed in low quantities. You can eat chickweed leaves and flowers raw, or you can cook them. However, it is recommended that you eat cooked chickweed because it contains low saponin levels.

Environment Where Found: Chickweed is a cool weather plant native to the European continent. However, the plant has been widely naturalized in the United States and most parts of the world. You will often find the chickweed plant in lawns and other areas with sufficient sunlight. The chickweed plant thrives in moist soil due to the unique conditions it provides.

Generally, this plant needs sufficient sunlight and areas with moderate air circulation. Even though the chickweed plant grows widely in most areas, you can grow it indoors. If you grow it for consumption purposes, don't use pesticides and other chemicals on it. This could make it dangerous for your health. When growing it indoors, ensure it has sufficient sunlight and keeps it in a moist place. This helps it grow abundantly.

Taste Profile: Chickweed tastes fresh and grassy. Its unique taste has also been likened to the flavor of corn silk. Apart from its fresh taste, chickweed has plenty of nutrients for our bodies. Consuming it supplies your body with vitamins, helping it protect itself against various illnesses. This goes a long way in keeping your health intact.

Harvesting and Usage: The cool spring weather is the best climate for chickweed plants. This plant grows rapidly through the months of March and April. When they are due for harvesting, you should use scissors to do so. Use your scissors to harvest the tender growth or simply trim off a couple of inches. This is the best way to harvest chickweed because it gives you the best quality products. Avoid harvesting young and underdeveloped chickweed plants because it could significantly damage its quality.

Recipe: Chickweed Pesto

There are many uses of chickweed. For instance, you can consume the plant directly to equip your body with important nutrients. Besides, you can use chickweed as a supplement in various dishes. This is helpful because chickweed introduces a unique flavor to your dish, making it tasty.

2-3 cloves minced garlic

½ cup cashews, walnuts, or pine nuts

1 tablespoon lemon juice

3 cups loosely packed chickweed

½ teaspoon salt

½ cup extra virgin olive oil

¼ cup freshly grated Parmesan cheese

¼ teaspoon black pepper (freshly ground)

1. Start by placing all ingredients into a food processor. Make sure that you process the content until it is smooth. This is vital because it helps break down the solid contents. You can also use a blender for this process. However, make sure that the chickweed is finely chopped before using a blender.

2. If the mixture is too thick, gradually drizzle tiny bits of olive oil to make it neutral. This is important because an overly thick mixture can affect the final product. You should also be careful not to add excessive olive oil when drizzling.

Notes: Ensure that you keep the mixture refrigerated to prevent it from going had. You can also eat or freeze within 3-4 days. Keep in mind that this is the period it could be contaminated. Safe storage is vital, for that matter.

Shoots, Shrubs, and Nuts

SOLOMON'S SEAL

Solomon's seal (*Polygonatum biflorum*) belongs to the asparagus (*Asparagaceae*) family, but in older field guides, it is categorized under the lily (*Liliaceae*) family. It is an herbaceous perennial rhizome with numerous circular scars or markings that are said to be similar to King Solomon's ancient Hebrew seal, hence the name. It is not to be confused with Solomon's plume.

Characteristics: The oval-shaped, parallel-veined leaves are alternate, with 10 to 25 individual leaves growing from the arching stems. The unbranched leaf stalks are measured at 0.5 meters to 1.5 meters in height.

The flowers are small and bell-like, measuring around 2 cm in diameter. They form pairs as they begin to sprout around the months of May to June. The flowers are typically white to pale green and are pendulous, hanging in 1 to 3 clusters like bells from a peduncle attached to the undersides of the arching stems. Afterward, these will turn into small, dark blue to black fruits that measure at around 0.5 to 1.25 cm each.

The rhizomes are disjointed and non-colonizing when the leaf stalks break. They leave scars that are reminiscent of the seal of King Solomon.

Environment: Solomon's seal is native to the eastern and central parts of North America but can also be seen growing in various parts of Canada. It thrives in dry to moist, rich woods and thickets, preferably under the shade.

Edible parts: The berries or fruits of this rhizome are toxic as they contain Anthraquinone. Albeit only with low toxicity, it will still cause stomach distress: diarrhea and vomiting. The shoots, however, are safe.

Since this is part of the asparagus family, the young shoots can be harvested, cooked, and served as you would asparagus. It is also not unlikely to see the shoots sliced and tossed in salads. The roots or the rhizomes of this plant are also edible. The Native Americans would regularly use it to make soup and bread as it is similar to a potato.

Recipe: Baked Solomon Seal Shoots

A bunch of Solomon's seal shoots (trimmed and cut)

Salt

Pepper

3 cloves of garlic (crushed)

Good olive oil

Parmesan cheese

1. Preheat your oven at 425° F. In a baking dish, place your Solomon's seal shoots in and drizzle a generous amount of olive oil over it. Toss in the crushed garlic, salt, and parmesan cheese and mix well.

2. Next, arrange the shoots in a single layer. Sprinkle more parmesan cheese on top and bake it in the oven for 12 to 15 minutes or until they are tender. Serve.

HOPNISS

Hopniss (*Apios americana*) is also known as American groundnut, potato bean, groundnut, hodoimo, and Indian potato. Part of the legume (*Fabaceae*) family, it is a perennial vine native to the US with edible beans and tubers. It is not cultivated in the US but is in Japan, where it is a specialty in the prefecture of Aomori. Brought to Japan accidentally during the Meiji period, it is now part of their diet.

Characteristics: This legume is a nitrogen-fixing vine, similar to the autumn olive. It climbs and twists around other neighboring plants. The vine can grow up to 1 to 6 meters long with pinnate compound leaves that alternate and measure at 8 to 15 cm long, each with individual 5 to 7 smaller leaflets per leaf. The leaf edges are smooth.

The flowers' colors range from pink, purple, or red-brown and grow on spikes or in dense racemes of around 7.5 to 13 cm per head. These flowers will sprout from the same node where the base of the leaf emerges.

There are also edible pods that look like pea pods and are measured at around 5 to 130 mm each. When cooked, the seeds taste like green beans.

The tubers are small but can also grow to the size of a potato. These are "chained" to the roots, well-spaced, in a line - early explorers in the New World would later call them "rosary" as the tubers do look like beads on a string. They grow horizontally and are easier to harvest when the soil is dry and sandy.

Environment: The hopniss are easily found in North America and in the southern parts of Canada. It prefers damp areas, places near marshes, creeks, rivers, and ponds. As it only needs a partial sun, you can find them near the edges of the woods or in the woods itself, where it is damp but still has enough sun coming through. It thrives in soil that is sandy loam. These have good drainage and can allow the tubers to grow freely while keeping in enough water.

When you are planning to look for this in the wild, be sure to know what poison sumac, poison ivy, and western poison ivy look like. These plants grow near each other as they thrive in the same environments. When you do see a hopniss in the wild, there are chances that you would also see one of these three poisonous plants nearby.

The leaves and the flowers of the hopniss when young can look like poison sumac to the untrained eye. So I suggest that you just move along and find a hopniss that is far away from the poisonous plants because touching any part of these plants, even the tubers, can cause similar distress.

Edible parts: The tubers and the peas are edible. The tubers of a hopniss plant are harvested during the fall seasons and be kept in storage until the next spring months arrive. It is like that of a potato in taste and mouthfeel, but it will have a nuttier bite to it as well as a finer texture. Although it is easy to find recipes that say these tubers can be eaten raw, I would advise against them. These tubers contain harmful protease inhibitors that are usually used in drugs for aids and HIV. But they are denatured when the tubers are well cooked. That said, the tubers are found to contain high levels of protein, around 3 times as much of those in potatoes, as well as amino acids, calcium, and iron.

They would need to be peeled and cooked like potatoes, so it is better to harvest only the medium-sized ones as the bigger ones will taste woodier, and the smaller ones will be harder to peel. They work best in stews or when fried like potatoes.

Recipe: Mashed Hopniss

2 cups of hopniss (washed, peeled, and chopped)

1 clove of garlic (mashed)

A quarter of a cup of milk

2 tablespoons of butter

Salt

Pepper

Half a cup of Parmesan cheese

1. Place hopniss in a steamer and steam for 10 to 15 minutes until it is tender. Let the hopniss cool down for a few minutes before mashing it with a fork or a potato masher.

2. In a small saucepan, bring the milk, garlic, butter, and parmesan cheese to a simmer on medium heat. Take it off the heat immediately to prevent the milk from curdling. Pour this over the

mashed hopniss and mix thoroughly. Season with salt and pepper to taste. Serve while hot.

CATTAIL

Cattail (*typha latifolia*) or bulrushes belong to the family of plants that is simply called the cattail family or *typhaceae*. It is native to the Northern and Southern parts of America as well as Africa, Europe, Canada, and Eurasia. It is considered a weed and invasive in Hawaii and Australia. Aside from being edible, it can be used to make various handicrafts as well as a primitive torch when the soft and fluffy heads are dipped in oil or fat.

Characteristics: The cattail is a perennial and has a stout stem often growing in dense clusters near wet places. The brown cylindrical formation on top during spring and the white downy mass of seeds it produces during autumn is easily distinguishable even for beginners.

The plant can grow up to 1.5 to 3 meters in height and have broad leaves that are 2 to 3 cm in length and 1 to 2 cm in width. The long, pale gray-green tapering leaves are basal, flat, and linear, which are thick and ribbon-like and, when dried, are used to make mats and baskets.

When young, the shoots will emerge in early spring on top of long and stout stalks that are unbranched. The fluffy brown heads of the cattail are often called "cigars." These "cigars" are female flowers that consist of thousands of minuscule seeds. Above the female flowers is the stiminate, a thin yellow spike that is the male flower. When fertilized during the autumn months, the flower heads open and scatter the cottony seeds.

Environment: The cattail grows in freshwater and prefers the moist and wet areas of swamps, thickets, and ditches. Their roots will go into the water until around 20cm deep but can also grow in soil that is just damp enough even when there is no water. Due to this, they are considered as signs of a transitional environment where dry land meets the wetlands. They are considered invasive in some parts as they can spread quickly over wetlands.

Edible parts: What people see as a weed is, in truth, a really useful plant. Almost every part of a cattail can be used or ingested in one way or another. The young stalks are edible and can be eaten raw or cooked like asparagus. Cooked, they taste a little like asparagus, raw they can be closer to cucumbers. The leaves are a great addition to salads. The female flowers should be picked when they are still green and young. It can be roasted and eaten as you would corn. As for the rhizomes, the outer spongy layer should be removed as they are inedible.

What is left should be white and firm - a little fibrous, but they can be dried and ground into flour. The pollen can also be used as a thickener in stews and hearty soups. The male flower produces copious amounts of pollen only in the first few weeks of spring. To harvest, simply shake the pollen off the flower head into a container. If kept airtight, it can be stored for weeks.

Medically, cattails have been used for centuries by the Native Americans. The roots can be pounded and applied to sores and wounds. The fluffy cottony mass of the matured female flowers is applied to burns as well as used to avoid chafing. The young flower heads are said to be able to help stop diarrhea.

The fully white mass that is reminiscent of cotton can also be used for insulation and bedding centuries before. When mixed with ash and lime, it can produce cement that is said to be harder than marble. Other than that, the leaves can be used for countless other uses, like that of palm leaves.

Recipe: Cattail on the Cob with Pasta

10 young cattail female flower heads

4 cloves of garlic (mashed)

Salt

1 tablespoon of butter

Olive oil

Pepper

Dried herbs of your choice

Pasta (for 1 person)

1 egg yolk

Parmesan cheese

1. Boil pasta until al dente. Take it out and drain while keeping a portion of the pasta water.

2. Place a skillet in medium-high heat. When hot enough, pour olive oil in along with the mashed garlic. Sauté until fragrant but not browned. Toss in the young cattail flowers. Cook until the cattail flower is tender but still toothsome.

3. Add in the drained pasta. Give the pan a shake and mix to coat the pasta with the garlic-infused oil. Add the butter in and season with salt and pepper. If the pasta is too dry, add the starchy pasta water by the spoonful.

4. Beat the egg yolk and combine it with the parmesan cheese. Take the pasta off the heat and wait for the heat to dissipate for a minute or so before pouring in the egg yolk mixture. Wait until the heat is low enough to not cook the eggs like scrambled eggs but still hot enough to melt the parmesan cheese. Serve while it is still hot with a few sprinklings of dried herbs on top.

AMERICAN HAZELNUT

American hazelnut (*Corylus americana*) is a deciduous shrub from the birch (*Betulaceae*) family. These are the wild and native hazelnuts that taste like the hazelnuts that can be usually seen in grocers but smaller. This species of hazelnut is not cultivated and is used mostly for ornamental and landscaping purposes. It is one of the varieties used to cultivate the Arbor Day Farm hybrid hazelnuts.

Characteristics: The American hazelnut spreads by sending suckers up from the rhizomes beneath the soil that are located 10 to 15 cm below the surface. It is medium to large-sized, multi-stemmed with long branches that grow outward, forming a dense circular crown. The crown spreads to measure at around 3 to 4.5 meters in diameter, with the whole shrub reaching the heights of 2.5 to 5 meters.

During the spring months, the shrub produces clusters of male staminate. These are yellow-brown in color and are pendulous; they hang like tiny bracelets of around 4 to 8 cm in length. Each cluster has 2 to 5 small female flowers or pistillates wrapped in the brackets of a bud with just the red styles protruding. Over the fall and winter months, the male staminate will turn into a flower with 4 stamens and 2 bracts.

The female flowers, when mature, turn into long edible nuts that are around 1.25 cm in diameter. The slightly egg-shaped nuts are wrapped in a thin brown husk-like pair of bracts and ripen in the months of July through October.

Environment: The American hazelnut is often used as an ornamental plant in gardens as hedges or a green screen. It is native to Southern Wisconsin but can also be found growing in the central and eastern parts of the US and in some portions of Canada. You can find them growing in well-drained loamy soil with full or partial sun. They are slightly drought and shade tolerant, but the hazelnut yield would not be as abundant during those conditions. It is not as commercially viable as that of the commercially cultivated European hazelnuts.

Edible parts: The nuts are a favorite of squirrels and other wildlife, so it is suggested to gather them up while the bracts are still green. The nuts are edible even when raw and have a sweet praline flavor accompanying them when roasted.

Recipe: American Hazelnut Praline Paste

2 cups of American hazelnut

1 and a quarter cup of white granulated sugar

Salt

3 tablespoons of water

1. Remove the skins or the bracts of the American hazelnut and toast them in a skillet on medium to high heat for 5 to 15 minutes. They will start smelling fragrant and develop brown spots here and there.

2. Make the caramel by combining the water and sugar in a saucepan. Cover and let the sugar melt under medium to high heat. Do not stir. When the sugar has melted and has developed a rich amber color, take it off the heat and pour it over a baking tray lined with baking papers. Let the caramel cool down completely before breaking it apart by hand or with a knife.

3. Using a food processor, blend the American hazelnuts and caramel shards together. It will turn into powder for the first few minutes, but when you reach the 5 to 10-minute mark, it will start to clump up because of the oils inside the nut. Blend until smooth. When kept in an airtight container, it can keep for a month.

Recipe: American Hazelnut Praline Truffles

A cup of roasted American hazelnuts

A cup of American hazelnuts praline paste

A cup of chopped up dark chocolate

1. Place the American hazelnuts praline paste in the fridge for a few hours to overnight to let it harden.

2. When the praline paste is hard enough, roll it into a ball, flatten it and place a whole roasted American hazelnut in the middle before covering it with the praline paste. Refrigerate the praline balls to harden overnight.

3. To temper the dark chocolate, prepare your double boiler or place a metal bowl over simmering water. Do not let the bottom of the bowl touch the simmering water. Melt two-thirds of the chopped chocolate, slowly stirring with a rubber spatula while keeping an eye on the temperature. Do not let the temperature go past 120°F.

4. When all of the chocolate has melted, take it off the heat and stir in the remaining ⅓ of the chocolate to melt. Once it reaches 82°F, place it back over the simmering water. Reheat until it reaches 88°F to 91°F, then turn off the heat.

5. Tempered chocolate, when spread thin over a piece of wax paper, should dry quickly and have a glossy finish. It should not have any streaks. It must be used while it is still liquid and hot. Re-temper it if it hardens by redoing the 2nd re-tempering.

6. Take the praline balls out of the fridge and quickly dip them into the tempered chocolate before letting it rest on a baking sheet. Allow the chocolate shells to harden before serving.

GINKGO

Ginkgo Biloba, otherwise known as just ginkgo, is a tree native to China. In its order *Ginkgoales*, which appeared 290 million years ago, Ginkgo Biloba is the only tree left that is extant, and also, unfortunately, it is listed as endangered. We can only find the other members of this family by looking through fossil records that go back to the middle Jurassic period. Because of this, it has claimed the title of being the oldest living tree in the world and is often called the living fossil. It is said that in Japan and China, one can find ginkgo trees that are up to 5,000 years old. It was brought over in 1794 and is now commonly used for landscaping in the New World.

It is not unlikely to hear people pronounce it as "gink-ko," and it is not surprising that ginkgo is an accepted alternative spelling for the tree. It is also said the word ginkgo is a misspelling of its Japanese name, *ging-Kyo* meaning silver apricot.

Characteristics: Ginkgos are large trees that can easily reach heights of 20 to 35 meters and reportedly even up to 50 meters - their spreads on mature trees reach 9 to 12 meters. The trunk of the ginkgo is covered with a cork-textured and fissured bark that gains deep furrows and a deeper brown color the older it gets.

Young trees would usually grow tall and slender, with the crown growing broader, longer, and more angular as it matures. The branches are erratic and grow in shoots accompanied with regularly spaced, unlobed leaves. These are occasionally deeply rooted, making them highly resistant to the outside elements. The shorter shoots grow slowly - around 2 cm for several years because of their short internodes.

The leathery green leaves are shaped like fans and grow in clusters from the tip of the short and stout shoots or spaced out and alternating along the branches. They are measured at 5 to 10 cm in length and around 16 cm in width, resembling the leaflets you would see on the maidenhair ferns. The leaves are also often divided into two lobes, separated by a notch at the center. Two parallel veins radiate and split out to the leaf edges from the stem. When autumn arrives, the leaves take on a bright shade of yellow that is prized for their beauty in Asia.

Ginkgo flowers do not appear until the tree reaches about 2 to 4 decades old. Since the trees are dioecious, some trees may just choose to exclusively bear male flowers while others are filled with only female ones. The yellow flowers bloom in April.

The fruit-like seed has a fleshy outer layer and measures 1.5 to 2 cm in length. It is yellow-brown in color and soft but smells like vomit when it drops off the tree. Harvest the seeds around autumn. You can squeeze the seeds into a bag while wearing gloves to keep the fleshy fruit's stink off your hands. Otherwise, if you are fortunate enough to have ginkgo trees near you. You can wait until February or March arrives. When the fleshy fruit has been worn away by the passage of time and naked ginkgo nuts are waiting for you under the tree.

Environment: Two million years ago, the population of the ginkgo trees shrank. They used to be widespread, with fossils of its leaves being found all the way in North Dakota, but their range shrank, and for years they were only growing in a small area in China.

Today the ginkgo trees are the only plant species that are older than the dinosaurs. They evolved in a time when ferns and cycads were abundant. These formed low and dense canopies along with the streamside or disturbing environments. The ginkgo trees adapted by producing large seeds and shot up to heights of 10 meters or more before spreading out its canopy. In this sense, the modern ginkgo trees are not unlike their fossilized brethren - they grow near streams and rivers in soils that are well-drained and have ample water. They grow slowly and reproduce late, which are opposite traits of what other plant species living in disturbed environments do.

In a rare case, humans are the reason why the tree still exists today. Due to its connection to Buddhism and its seeds having purported medicinal qualities, it was cultivated by ancient monks and grown for their seeds in China. Wild and undomesticated ginkgo trees, however, are thought to be extinct until recently, when studies suggest that there might be a copse somewhere in the mountains of southwestern China.

Fortunately, these beautiful trees are tenacious and easily propagate with just their seed. It should be worth mentioning that 6 trees survived the atomic bomb attack in Hiroshima when other living things did not make it. They were growing just 1 to 2 kilometers away from the bomb site.

The trees adapt well to urban environments. It grows happily in the middle of bustling cities tolerating pollution and cramped spaces well. Today, they can be found from lining the streets of Manhattan and Washington DC to making appearances in bonsai exhibitions, making people marvel at their autumnal yellow leaves.

Edible parts: The outer flesh is unpleasant, smells like vomit, and shouldn't be eaten, but once taken off, the seeds or nuts are edible. Readers, be warned, though - there are people allergic to ginkgo seeds.

The seeds are medicinal and can help with memory retention. Because of this, the seeds are very popular in Asia. Markets there sell the seeds shelled, cleaned, and packaged. It is a regular ingredient added to various dishes. The leaves are astringent but can be made into tea by simply boiling them.

Recipe: Chicken Soup with Lotus Root and Ginkgo Nuts

*Lotus roots can be bought in your nearby specialty grocer as well as in an Asian market near you.

A handful of ginkgo nuts (around 3 to 4 per person should be enough)

A few slices of chopped lotus roots (Roughly a cup)

500 g of chicken (bone-in for that extra tasty broth)

4 cloves of garlic (crushed)

Salt

1. Place the chicken in a pot with water and let it boil for a minute. Drain the chicken and throw the water out.

2. In a new flat bottomed pot, heat some oil and toss in the crushed garlic. Sauté until fragrant and tender but not browned. Add in the drained chicken; brown the chicken for a little bit before adding water. Pour enough water, so it covers the chicken, then add in the ginkgo nuts and chopped lotus root.

3. Cover the pot and let it simmer in low heat for 30 to 40 minutes. After simmering in low heat, uncover and season with a dash of salt. Let it simmer in medium heat for 10 minutes before turning the heat off. Serve while hot.

RED MAPLE

Red maple (*acer rubrum*) has many names: soft maple, Carolina red maple, Water maple, Drummond red maple, and scarlet maple, among others. It's a deciduous tree that is widespread in the central and eastern parts of North America as well as Canada. When young, it can be at times considered invasive in young forests. Although cultivated for its medium to high-quality lumber and maple syrup, it is mostly planted for ornamentation in North America.

Characteristics: The red maple is a short-lived tree, rarely reaching the age of 150 or older. The bark on young trees is smooth to touch and has a light grey color. As it matures, the bark darkens and develops fine scaly plates that break up. It is a medium-sized tree and reaches heights measuring 27 to 41 meters. Height can vary greatly depending on the environment - red maples found in thickly wooded forests have a tendency to be shorter. The trunk on mature trees can reach diameters of 46 to 88 cm and has been reported to reach 153 cm at times.

In a forest, the trunks can grow some distance without any branches. Meanwhile, in open areas, these trees grow short with branches hanging low and a rounder crown. The smaller branches are red with small lenticels and blunt green or red buds in the fall and winter months. The leaves on matured trees average 9 to 11 cm in length. They grow opposite each other with jagged edges and simple palmate lobes numbering at 3 to 5. On the upper surface, the leaves are green, while the undersides are white or hairy with red leaf stalks that are around 10 cm long. In autumn, the leaves turn a bright shade of red or yellow-orange.

Flowers are small and hang in clusters appearing in the late winter months to early spring before the leaves can sprout. After the flowers, the fruits appear, also in clusters in late spring to the early summer months. These are light brown or yellow samaras measuring 1.25 to 2 cm in length.

Environment: The red maple is a common sight in the eastern parts of North America, in some parts of Canada, as well as in select parts of Europe. Although it prefers well-drained and moist habitats, the red maple can grow in almost any type of environment. The diverse range on where it can grow - from swamps and peat bogs to dry ridges - and its prolific seed-producing capabilities make the red maple highly adaptive.

Edible parts: The leaves, inner bark, seeds, as well as sap of the red maple are edible. The seeds can be eaten raw as well as toasted. If raw, it is suggested to soak them in water to eliminate any trace of bitterness first. The inner bark, used by the Native Americans as a remedy for inflamed eyes and cataracts, can be eaten cooked or raw. The leaves taste best when they are young.

Red maples are also cultivated for their sap or syrup, though not as much as the black maple or the hard maple. It will need to be tapped before the first buds sprout; else, there would be a noticeable change in the taste of the syrup. That is in spring, making the maple syrup season for the red maple rather short.

Recipe: Red Maple Chips

A handful of fresh and cleaned red maple leaves

1 egg

3 tablespoons of panko or dried bread crumbs

Maple syrup

1. In a small saucepan, heat enough oil - around 1 and a half-inch from the bottom - until smoking. Or you can insert the tip of a wooden stick or chopstick in the oil. If the tip bubbles, then it's hot enough.

2. Beat the egg and pour it into a small shallow pan. On another pan, pour panko.

3. Make sure the maple leaves are cleaned and dry. Dip both sides in the egg mixture first before dipping and coating it with panko. For extra crunch, it is recommended that you repeat this step twice.

4. Slowly slide it in the hot oil. Fry for a few minutes on both sides until the coating is lightly browned. Then, let it drain on a kitchen towel. Serve with a drizzle of maple syrup on top.

PINE NUTS

Nuts make a very rich food selection for those who are into foraging. When we first started foraging, we found it easy to use fruits and nuts as compared to other greens. This is because nuts can be made without much processing.

Also known as *pignoli*, pine nuts are products of pine trees. When pine trees mature, the seeds are harvested and used for food, which is what we call pine nuts. The Food and Agriculture Organization has categorized edible pine nuts into 29 species. Twenty of these are traded locally, while the others are ideally foraged by those who farm them.

Characteristics: With over 29 species of edible pine nuts, it is difficult to pin down the true characteristics of this plant. The popular pine tree is the limber pine, which is a small to medium-size tree that grows to 40 feet tall and has a stem diameter of about 20 inches. This tree is a true representation of the other pine species due to its versatility in terms of growth.

The pine tree is extremely slow in terms of growth. Some of the species of this tree may take as long as a hundred years to grow to maturity. However, they also have a very long lifespan that compensates for their slow growth. Pine trees can live well over a thousand years.

Edible Parts: The edible part of a pine tree is the pine nut. The nuts are rich in certain vitamins and nutrients. Experts say that they are rich sources of thiamine, Vitamin B1 protein. The nuts themselves are located within the cones of pine trees.

Environment Where Found: Trees that take hundreds of years to mature, it is impossible to tie them to one climate or soil profile. These are trees that adapt to soil and climate hangs very fast and can grow in most parts of the world. Pine trees thrive in the harsh and cold climates of northeast Siberia but also flourish with a warm tropical climate. They even grow in hot and dry deserts like the Nevada and Mexico desserts.

Due to their resilience to climatic conditions, pine nuts are among the plants that have been used by humans for a long time. Humans have been foraging this sweet nut for thousands of years, as recorded in history.

Taste profile: Nuts are not necessarily sweet foods. They are rich in fats and have a buttery texture and flavor. When you crunch a few pine nuts individually, you may experience an almost tasteless buttery feeling. However, they offer a resinous pine-like flavor.

Pine nuts are not good to be eaten raw or alone. They work well when they are served with other ingredients. When combined with other ingredients, the nuts may have a mild sweetness as an aftertaste.

Harvesting and Usage: If you are lucky enough to have a mature pine tree in your garden to forage, you should harvest the nuts and try them out. Although you can harvest from different types of pinyon trees, it is recommended to only harvest from mature ones. Since some trees provide a better harvest than others, choose one that is well matured.

Make sure you harvest your pine cones before they open. Once the cones open, birds may pick away the nuts leaving behind empty shells. To ensure that you get value for money, it is recommended to harvest pine cones that are well matured and dried but not ones that are already open.

To harvest your pine cones, grab one with your hand and twist its position to pluck it off its branch. The pine cone should come off easily. If it is not dry, you may want to let them dry before opening the cones to enjoy your nuts.

Recipe: Toasted Pine Nuts

Pine nuts are very popular in most American homes. The only difference between foraged nuts and what Americans use is that foraged nuts are not processed; you will have to undertake the processing steps yourself. If you are into foraging, you may realize that processing foods at a home level are much fun. More interesting is the many options you have when it comes to developing custom recipes. Most importantly, processing your pine nut will also give you an opportunity to enjoy all-natural food without having to add chemicals to it.

1 cup of freshly harvested pine nuts- should be dry

1 tablespoon of olive oil

salt for flavoring- optional

<u>To toast pine nuts in the oven:</u> Toasting pine nuts in the oven is quite a simple process that does not take plenty of time. Below are the steps to follow:

1. Preheat your oven to about 350 degrees Celsius.

2. Line your baking sheet with parchment paper or aluminum foil.

3. Toast your pine nuts in oil and add some salt if you wish.

4. Arrange them in the baking sheet above and bake until brown. Make sure you stir your nuts occasionally to avoid a situation where they charred.

5. Remove the nuts from the oven and use as desired. They can be taken directly as cereal with milk or be taken as snacks. You can also prepare a pin nut paste that can be used in cooking other dishes. The nuts cooked in this recipe can be stored for up to 1 week.

To toast pine nuts on the stove: If you do not wish to use your oven, you may also do your cooking the old-fashioned way. With this recipe, you can also use a stove to prepare your nuts.

1. Toss your nuts in oil and salt if you wish to. Heat the pine nuts in a skillet over medium heat until they are slightly browned. Remember to constantly stir your nuts since they may easily get chard on the stove.

2. After about 5 to 7 minutes, your nuts should be lightly browned and fragrant. Remove from the skillet and use them as you desire. These nuts can be stored in an airtight jug for use for up to a week.

3. With that, you have your recipe for pine nuts. I have been gathering pine nuts for as long as I can remember in the field. Unfortunately, the rare nuts are not easy to come across; we have a few trees where we stay, but we only manage to get a few nuts around the year.

SCUPPERNONG

Scuppernong or wild grapes are available in most parts of the US, especially the southern states where they grow naturally. Most Americans interchange the terms scuppernong muscadine. Although they are not the same, they both refer to different varieties of wild grapes. Scuppernong specifically originated in North Carolina in the 7thcentury and has so far been domesticated by many farmers.

Scuppernong can be cultivated or found in the wild. If you choose to farm yours, ensure that you are in a region with sufficient sunlight. Also, avoid the use of chemicals such as pesticides that may affect your final output.

Characteristics: Scuppernongs are climbing plants. They grow along the fence or may need support from other plants. Those who farm them provide support to allow the plant to spread. Some species have tall stems that are vital in pollination.

Edible Parts: Although we only think of scuppernongs as fruits, they can also serve other purposes. Before I started foraging, I did not know that their leaves were edible. Like most of us who are used to store-bought foods, many people have no idea that scuppernong leaves can make a good salad.

If you will be eating the leaves, choose the young fresh ones. These are tender and have a flavor close to that of grapes. The other part that is edible is the fruit. The entire fruit, including the skin, is edible; however, people may choose to discard the skin while others may eat the entire fruit. Those who do not prefer eating the skin squeeze the berry out before eating.

Environment where Found: Scuppernongs are named after the Scuppernong River, which is located in North Carolina. As already mentioned, this fruit is native to the southern United States, specifically North Carolina. The grapes were originally found in growing wild in the State in the 17th century before farmers started producing them commercially.

If you are into farming Scuppernongs, make sure you reside in a state where there is sufficient sunshine throughout the year. These fruits thrive in regions where there is sufficient sunshine, humidity, and cool air at night. All southern states, including South and North

Carolina, Georgia, Kentucky, and others, are ideal for farming Scuppernong.

Taste Profile: The Scuppernong is a very sweet fruit with intense sweetness like a concord grape. The Scuppernong also has very thick and spicy skin that tastes like plums. Although it is not a must to eat the skin, some people love the skin for its flavor.

Harvesting and Usage: Unlike some types of grapes that are harvested once they are mature and ripened, the Scuppernong is only harvested when it is ripe. Each fruit is harvested individually since it must be touched. If you harvest raw fruits, they will not ripen and will end up in waste.

Normally, the fruits are harvested in their third season of growth. Grapes usually mature from early August to September. Most farmers let the fruits fall by themselves when they are ready for harvesting. However, if the fruits are ripe, the best way to harvest in mass is by shaking the tree. The fruits that are ripe will easily fall down for picking.

Recipe: Scuppernong Jelly Recipe

While there are many ways to use your fruits, one of the best ways is to prepare jelly. The jelly can be applied to bread and other dishes you may enjoy at home.

2 quarts of scuppernong grapes that are washed and stemmed

1/2 a cup of water

3 cups of sugar

1. Gather the above ingredients and prepare a boiling water bath. Place a few small plates in the freezer for the jelly test.

2. Squeeze the pulp out of the hulls and keep the pulp and hulls in separate containers.

3. Chop out hulls and place them in a pan with 1/2 a cup of water.

4. Immerse the hulls until tender while stirring occasionally. If it gets sticky, add a bit of water.

5. In a different saucepan, cook the pulp until it softens. Remove from heat and press the pulp through a sieve to remove the seeds.

6. In a large pan, now combine the pulp and hulls and add about 3/4 cup of sugar for each cup of the fruit mixture. Bring the mixture to a boil and cook until thickened. This should take approximately 1 to 20 minutes. Continue to stir until the mixture is even and thickened.

7. On one of the chilled plates, drop a spoon of the hot jam. Let it rest for about 20 seconds. When you tilt your plate, your jam should be thick enough to move slightly but not too thin that it runs. If your jam is runny, continue cooking while stirring until you have a thick jelly.

8. Now, transfer your jelly into sterilized jars. Make sure you leave about 1.4-inch headspace.

9. Now, carefully wipe the residue from jar mouths using a towel moistened in boiled water.

10. Cover the jars with seals and rings and let your jar sit in a hot water bath for about 15 minutes.

With that, you have prepared your all-sweet and tasty scuppernong jelly that can be applied to bread and other pastries. This is just one of the many ways in which you can use your fruits. Remember that both the leaves and fruits are edible. There are many other recipes you will find that are ideal for this fruit. We currently do not have scuppernong in our locality, but a friend brought us some last summer, and we had fun with this recipe.

GREEN ONIONS (SCALLIONS)

Scallions, popularly referred green onions are vegetables belonging to the genus Allium. These vegetables are very common and popular in most households across the US. Scallions have a similar taste to bulb onions, except that their taste is mild. They are close relatives to onions, leek, shallot, and Chinese onions.

Green onions are grown in most parts of the world. We have a large part of the manor dedicated to growing green onions. They grow quite first and can be reused for a long time.

Characteristics: Scallions are above the ground vegetable with stiff white stalks. They grow to about 3 feet in highest at maximum, but some can remain as low as 1 foot above the ground. They are identified by their long tender green leaves.

The stalks of the onion are less than one inch in diameter. The onion usually does not have bulb roots, as is the case with others. Green onions have stringy white roots. The onions grow in bunches and are usually harvested young.

In essence, green onions are just regular bulb onions that are harvested before they attain maturity. This prevents them from forming the bulb. For this reason, they are mild in taste than other types of onion.

Edible Parts: Almost everything on a green onion is edible. Green onions are made up of four main parts; the long, tender green leaves, the white stalk, the small bulb, and the thin veil-like roots. The vein roots are the only part that is not edible on the onion. The rest are edible, including the stalk; the leaves and stalk can be eaten while raw or cooked. They taste just like onions, except that they are slightly mild.

Environment where found: Green onions are found virtually everywhere. Originally, the onions were grown in Asia, but they have spread to all parts of the world. If you wish to grow your scallions in the backyard, make sure you have the right soil type and access to the required weather. The plant thrives in full sun and requires fertilizing. You will have to add some fertilizer to the soil before planting your scallions.

Scallions do well in organic soils that are well-drained. Space your scallions 2 to 3 inches apart in rows. These species can grow across the US but will do much better in the southern states.

Taste Profile: Green onions have a juicy and crisp grassy taste. They are sweet and slightly pungent in flavor. They taste just like full grow onions except that they are mild.

Harvesting and Usage: Scallions are ready to harvest as soon as the leaves are long enough for use. People harvest the leaves at different stages. From as early as one month, you may be able to harvest your onions. Ideally, scallions should be harvested early morning when the dew is still on the leaves. This way, you get the freshest of the harvest. To harvest, loosen the soil around the plant and gently pull it out of the ground

Recipe: Steam Grilled Green Onions

Green onions are an integral part of everyday cooking. Essentially, green onions can be used as spices in the same way we use mature onions. In this manner, green onions can be used in cooking countless meals. Any meal where you use bulb onions can also be cooked with scallions. Besides their use as a spice, green onions can be used as. In this manner, the onion is cooked as part of the meal rather than being used as a spice.

Below is a simple recipe we learned while at the manor that will be helpful for those foraging green onions.

Steam grilled onions are quite delicious and easy to prepare. With this recipe, the onions are part of the main dish rather than being used as a spice. Below is the detailed recipe.

12 cleaned and rinsed green onions with the ends trimmed

2 cloves of garlic, minced

2 tablespoons of butter sliced into small pieces

A pinch of salt and ground black pepper to taste

1. Preheat your grill to medium-low

2. Cut a sheet of aluminum foil to 12 x 15 inches and arrange the onions side-by-side at the center of the foil.

3. Sprinkle some garlic all over the onions and add salt with pepper.

4. Add the butter on top of the onions with the onions flat on the foil. Fold the aluminum foil to make a sealed cooking pouch.

5. Place the foil packet on the grill but keep it away from the main heat source and allow your green onions to steam for about 5 to 7 minutes.

6. Once your onions are ready, remove them from the foil and serve while hot. These onions can be taken alongside other vegetables be served with pasta or any other dish of your choice. They are quite tasty and will also enrich your body with essential vitamins.

ACORNS

Acorn is a fruit of the oak tree. Oak trees are the flowering plant genus Quercus that fall under the Fagaceae family. Normally, acorns contain a single seed (in rare cases, some have two seeds) enclosed in a leathery, tough shell. You will also notice some in a cup-shaped cupules. Acorns have several uses and are very important to living species, especially animals.

They are a source of food for many animals, including squirrels, birds, bears, and deer. Based on the harmony and cohesiveness of nature, many of these animals also serve as dispersal agents for the acorn plant. They help spread its germination range to other areas beyond its parent tree. As much as the acorn plant is known to be a source of food for animals, humans can also consume it. However, you need to be careful not to eat too much of it because it could lead to stomach upsets.

Characteristics: Generally, acorns are usually surrounded by a woody cupule. They mature within a short time of between one to two seasons. It is important to note that the appearance of acorns varies depending on the oak species. These plants are very important because they provide food for wildlife and other animals. You can also use them to fatten poultry and swine. Keep in mind that these plants contain bitter tannins, with the level of this substance varying from one species to another. Since tannins, which are originally plant polyphenols, interfere with an animal's ability to metabolize proteins, consumers must establish ways to obtain nutrients found in acorns.

In some cases, animals preferentially choose acorns with fewer tannins. This helps them break down acorns easily and obtain the necessary nutrients. It also reduces the risk of injury due to limited thorns. High consumption of tannins is very dangerous to animals. For instance, when tannins are metabolized in a cow, the resulting acid can cause kidney failure and ulceration. This only makes the condition worse. Therefore, you need to be careful with the amount of acorn your cow consumes.

Edible Parts: Acorns can be eaten. You can eat them as a whole, grind them up into acorn flour or meal, or crush them into mush to extract oil. Once you have successfully removed tannins from raw acorns, you can roast them for about 15 minutes and sprinkle them with salt to make a delicious snack. Besides, you can use roasted acorns to make a delicious snack called acorn brittle.

This tasty meal is similar to peanut brittle and comes with plenty of nutritional value. You can also make acorn coffee, which is a caffeine-free substitute for regular coffee. Making it is easy. Start by slowly roasting acorns over low heat for around two hours. Make sure you move them regularly to ensure every area is covered. Then, remove them from the heat and let them cool down. After that, grind them thoroughly.

This is vital because it ensures easy consumption. If you don't want to go through the tedious process of removing tannins from fresh acorns, you can purchase acorn flour from local supermarkets or online retail shops. They come fresh with no tannins, making them ideal for consumption. You can use the flour for various purposes, including baking.

Taste Profile: The acorn plant tastes a little bitter. It also has an intense flavor. Apart from that, nothing separates them from other types of nuts, such as pecans or almonds. This means that in terms of flavor, acorns are almost similar to other nuts. Besides, the texture is similar to other nuts — foods with acorn flavor are crunchy but not difficult to chew on. In fact, you find acorns almost similar to chestnuts. Keep in mind that chestnuts have a distinctive texture and flavor.

This is why it is important to consider certain facts when deciding what to do with acorns. For instance, you should consider the ingredients in the dish you plan to prepare. You can use acorn flour to bake all kinds of goodies; however, it is important to note that this might not work if many sweet spices or chocolates are involved in the recipe. Too many sweet ingredients can significantly affect the effects of acorn flour on your dish.

Harvesting and Usage: The first thing you need to do when harvesting acorns is finding a live oak tree. Experts recommend that you go for a white oak tree due to its unique flavor. Any species of oak tree will also work, like black oak trees, red oak trees, and others. It is important to note that there are many varieties of acorns, and some are way better than others when it comes to nutrient supply. This is because some have more tannins than others, making them overly bitter. When harvesting acorns, the goal is to find plants with the least number of tannins.

This is important because the presence of too many tannins makes acorns extremely bitter. There are many uses of acorns. For instance, you can use them in place of nuts in recipes such as brownies and cookies. Besides, you can also use them in place of cornmeal in several recipes. It is vital to note that keeping acorn flour in a sealed container helps prolong its shelf life. For instance, if you store it in a freezer, it will be in good condition for several months.

A typical acorn meal contains oil, meaning it could turn rancid if you keep it in a warm place. If you plan to store whole acorns, dry them first. Do so by exposing them to direct sunlight for two to five days. Alternatively, you can dry them in a 175°C oven for 20 minutes. You should keep the oven door slightly open to allow moisture to escape. This is essential because the presence of moisture can affect dry acorns. After successfully drying acorns, they will remain safe to eat for several years.

Recipe: Acorn Brittle

Acorn brittle is an American classic that can satisfy any hungry mouth. It has almost the same taste as peanut brittle. The only difference is that it uses acorns instead! Acorn brittle has a wide range of nutrients that help keep your body in good condition. For instance, it supplies your body with carbohydrates that are vital for body health. You will also get proteins and a few vitamins.

100g roasted acorns

100g caster sugar

1. Start by leaching it with hot water. This is important because it helps keep it in good condition.

2. Then, tip the caster sugar into a solid saucepan over low heat. Avoid using excessive heat because it can affect the whole process.

3. Gently shake the pan immediately; sugar starts to melt and darken in color. This prevents sugar from sticking on the surface. When the sugar turns dark brown, add acorns and stir. You should do it gently to avoid any inconveniences.

4. Then, gently remove it from heat and pour it into a baking tray. Make sure that the baking tray is lined with greaseproof paper to avoid burning.

5. Lastly, leave it to cool down and harden. The best way to do so is by leaving it under room temperature. Alternatively, you can leave it at normal temperature but keep an eye on it to avoid melting.

CONCLUSION

The manor was opened to the public 5 years ago. From that time until now, we have seen a steady increase in guests and visitors coming in from different walks of life and from all parts of the world. We are deeply flattered and happy, of course.

From a simple arrangement of just me and my wife, our family has now grown to 4 members and a dog. We also now have docents coming in to help with the "living museum" - as my wife calls it - from the local art university. We stage talks about sustainability and the environment too for the regular townsfolk and guests.

There is something magical about being this much nearer to nature and being surrounded on all sides by the rustling of leaves and the smell of wet trees. The atmosphere brings so much calm and peace to our guests and us. Nature is so majestic and so giving that it just lets you stand there, and all the pent-up stress and tension from years of working just washes away.

We started out as a bed and breakfast that offers an immersive experience of a Victorian house, but since then, we have expanded and catered to the guests with bespoke meals gathered from the woods and gardens out back. It simply does not make sense that we do not make use of that cavernous kitchen on the back wing. Also, sharing what I've learned through the years just makes me glow inside, so this book was written as a companion - may it stoke your love for a freer life and, of course, foraging.

My parting words for you are these:

Once you've seen and read about some of the most common wild plants you can find in your local area, please take note of their edible parts and know-how to prepare and eat them. It doesn't at all mean that if a plant's seed is edible, the entire plant could also be ingested. There are plants out there whose stems and leaves can be toxic, but the flowers, when roasted, are extremely palatable.

This is why I espouse familiarity - you can not go into the woods and treat it like a store for the most part. Nature has rules and schedules, and not everything should bow to the whims of humankind. Everything has its time. For example, if you are planning to make elderberry jams for stocking, make a note of when the berries will ripen and proceed to the area with the correct tools and mindset with you at the right season. This way, you are prepared, and you can eliminate mistakes along the way. Know what plants are in season and forage accordingly.

Take only what you need. Human disturbance is the cause of a lot of species being extinct, plant or otherwise. Although there are a few out there that have managed to survive until now because of human cultivation, it doesn't always work out well for others.

Now, if you're thinking about the ginkgo trees, they do propagate easily, so cultivation is a good way to ensure the lineage of the species will not be stopping anytime soon. However, this truth does not hold well for others

Take the famous huckleberry in our country as an example. Botanists and biologists could not figure out how to cultivate this famous edible berry, and the same goes for silphium, an ancient plant that the Romans and the Greeks loved. It was so important back then that Julius Caesar stockpiled it in the treasury. It was said to be worth its weight in gold and was so important that they had its image engraved on their coins.

It was a lauded plant in antiquity, but it disappeared from history because of over-harvesting and overgrazing. Silphium is an example of one plant that could not be cultivated, even though the Romans tried to. All they could do was slowly watch this beloved herb fade away to extinction. It was gone by the 3rd or 2nd century BCE.

Our human brains are easy to trick. Do not be overconfident as you go into the woods. Foraging is already out of most people's comfort zones. You do not need to prove yourself and swagger into the woods carrying a knife, taking plants without double-checking. Always question yourself and the plant. Is this really a giant puffball mushroom? Cut it open and see for sure if the flesh is white and has no gills. You must always be a hundred percent sure of the wild food you are eating. Death by poisoning wild plants is not uncommon in America.

In that vein, when you do consume a wild plant, always keep a part of it untouched and uncooked. If the worst does happen, you can bring this to the ER, and they can quickly help you find an antidote.

Be a smart forager - do not believe in myths and old wives' tales. You cannot eat small parts of a poisonous plant in order for you to develop "immunity." If the field guide and everyone say it's inedible, do not try to eat it.

If you do plan to spend a large part of your day in the woods foraging, know what plants and fungi are in season, then pack and prepare accordingly. Bring several bags with you. It's better not to mix plants that have different properties. Some might be bitter raw or may be wrapped in a toxic outer layer. If so, keep this away from the more delicate and mild-tasting edibles. The same goes for medicinal plants too.

Lastly, take the universal edibility test. I did not want to place this at the beginning of the book, fearing readers might start putting things into their mouths and getting poisoned. But I'm writing this here in case you might ever find a need for it in the future.

Of course, your best chance of survival is always to stick to what you know. Life is not worth risking. This is for emergencies only, so please do not try this with just any plant you see.

It is a slow process, but follow the steps one by one and do not skip a step. If you do find yourself in a life or death situation up in the woods, this might just come in handy.

Separate the plant into parts - leaves, stems, flowers, roots, and buds. Pay attention to one plant part at a time.

If you smell it and it has a strong and unpleasant odor, it is not a good sign.

Next, you shall test for contact poisoning. For a few minutes, place a piece of the plant on your wrist or inner elbow where your skin is the thinnest and wait. If you develop rashes, burns, stings or any other unpleasant sensation, do not eat it.

If you feel nothing unpleasant on your skin after placing it on your inner elbow and wrist, move on to the next step and boil the plant.

After boiling, place the plant against your lips and let it stay there for a few minutes. If there's nothing, take a small bite and chew it. Do not swallow. Hold it in your mouth for 15 minutes. If you feel an unpleasant feeling in your mouth or if the plant tastes bitter or soapy, do not eat the plant.

If you do not feel any unpleasant sensation in your mouth, you can now swallow the plant and wait for several hours. If you do not feel anything bad happening inside your body, you can therefore assume that the plant might be edible.

You can now choose to repeat the test on the other plant parts to figure out which ones are safe to eat and which ones are not.

#########

Thank you so much for reading my book. I hope it has helped you in some way. Would you please leave a review online where you purchased this book? Thanks!

Printed in Great Britain
by Amazon